ELECTRIC RAILWAYS

AROUND SAN FRANCISCO BAY

VOLUME TWO

MARKET STREET RAILWAY - MUNICIPAL RAILWAY OF SAN FRANCISCO - NORTHWESTERN PACIFIC RAILROAD
PETALUMA & SANTA ROSA RAILROAD - SACRAMENTO NORTHERN RAILWAY
SAN FRANCISCO, NAPA & CALISTOGA RAILROAD - SHIPYARD RAILWAY

Compiled by Donald Duke

Golden West Books

ELECTRIC RAILWAYS AROUND SAN FRANCISCO BAY

Volume Two

Published by Golden West Books
San Marino, California 91118 U.S.A.

Library of Congress Catalog Card No. 99-046646
I.S.B.N. No. 0-87095-116-5

Library of Congress Cataloging-in-Publication Data

Duke, Donald, 1929-
Electric railways around San Francisco Bay / compiled by Donald Duke
p. cm.
Includes bibliographical references.
ISBN 0-87095-116-5
1. Electric railroads—California—San Francisco Bay Area. I. Title.

TF1025.S26 D85 2000 99-046646
385.5'09794'6—dc21 CIP

First Printing - March 2000
Second Printing - February 2003

Cover and Title Page Illustration

Market Street Railway's San Mateo interurban cars often raced Southern Pacific's commuter trains up and down this section of track. In this scene, interurban car No. 1244 has stopped at the Broadway Station to pick up mid-day passengers bound for San Francisco. Southern Pacific's San Francisco-San Jose commuter, and main line, is just behind the station at the left of this photograph. — DONALD DUKE COLLECTION

Golden West Books
P.O. Box 80250
San Marino, California • 91118-8250

This volume is dedicated
to
Charles D. Savage

Wire Chief for Western Union
railroad photographer, and a long time friend.

One of the most beautiful stations on the Northwestern Pacific's electric line was the modern depot at Ross. The depot featured a garden rivaling the landscaping of Marin County mansions. When rail service ended, the United States Post Office occupied the site, and the gardens were maintained. — Charles D. Savage

Table of Contents

Train No. 1, the *San Francisco Passenger,* left the Sacramento Northern station in Sacramento at 6:55 A.M., bound for San Francisco. At 9:19 A.M. Will Whittaker photographed her climbing through Redwood Canyon, just east of Havens. In 1937 this train terminated at the Key System pier terminal, with final destination at San Francisco via ferryboat. — Will Whittaker

Introduction

This is the second volume, and the last, in this series on the *Electric Railways Around San Francisco Bay.* I trust that those who have purchased this volume would also enjoy Volume One. At least you would have a complete set featuring the pictorial history of the electric railways of the San Francisco Bay. As was explained in the introduction of Volume One, all of this is based on what I remembered in 1939 and on subsequent visits. I have presented some history of when the roads began, and then brought the reader up to the time of the abandonment of service. It should be remembered that I did not take the majority of the illustrations shown in either volume. They are mainly the camera artistry of Harre Demoro and Charles D. Savage, plus many, many others. In the good old days we traded photographs, and these illustrations were from my collection.

Volume One started the alphabetic sequence of the *Electric Railways Around San Francisco Bay.* This volume picks up where Volume One left off. Presented here are the Market Street Railway, the Municipal Railway of San Francisco, Northwestern Pacific, Petaluma & Santa Rosa, the southern end of the Sacramento Northern, San Francisco & Napa Valley, and lastly the Shipyard Railway. Ah yes, the Shipyard Railway was a line whose equipment was nearly a half-century old when it was built!

Considering my age, I do not claim to have ridden or photographed all of these lines. I was in the San Francisco Bay area in 1939, and did not visit again until 1947. After that I made several safari's to the "city." Unfortunately, I did not get to see the Shipyard Railway in operation. I did, however, ride a two-car train set on an excursion over the Key System. It was quite an experience! I understand there is a two-car set still in existence at the Bay Area Electric Railroad Association's Western Railway Museum at Rio Vista Junction.

As for the Market Street Railway, it disappeared after my initial visit in 1939. I rode the "40-Line" between San Francisco and San Mateo on several occasions. It was impressive to see how fast the old cars moved. At the time I was using my grandfathers Kodak, and was unaware that a leak had appeared in the leather pull-out bellows, causing all of the photographs to have light streaks. The only good shot is the sign at Burlingame/Broadway which appears in this volume. I also rode the Market Street cars that raced down the four tracks of Market Street, but as to what line they were on is lost to the ages.

I have ridden all the lines of the San Francisco Municipal Railway any number of times, and photographed the system with Harre Demoro on two occasions. I rode one of the big blue cars last June (1999) on an excursion that was a side trip of the joint Railway & Locomotive Historical Society-National Railway Historical Society Convention. This formed a part of the California State Railroad Museum's celebration "Railfair 99." It was great to see people staring at the old battlewagon as it rolled down Market Street.

The tangerine colored blimps of the Northwestern Pacific are only a fuzzy memory. Way back in 1939, the family was invited to an old friends home in San Rafael for lunch. I remember riding the ferry to Sausalito, where a blimp was waiting which took us to San Rafael. Basically, all I remember is the bars across the windows which prevented me from sticking my head out. Apparently, there was a clearance problem.

I was too young to see the interurban operations on the Petaluma & Santa Rosa. The road's wood, center-entrance cars reminded me of the Jewett Car Company cars on the Charles City Western. Although electric freight operation continued until January 24, 1947, I never was able to get up to Petaluma, or Santa Rosa, to see and photograph the locomotives.

Bound for Mill Valley, this Northwestern Pacific interurban train is stopping at the Park Avenue station to let off a passenger. One more stop before the train will terminate at Mill Valley. There was little midday traffic in 1938 since the Mount Tamalpais & Muir Woods Railway trains ceased running to the summit of Mount Tamalpais. Note how the right-of-way is fenced in at the right, and the third rail is covered over with a wood shield. — Charles D. Savage

The Sacramento Northern mainline ran east on Shafter Avenue en route to Sacramento and Chico. My Cousin, Jack Lamborn, had a home on this tree-lined avenue. I thought how very exciting it was to have a railroad going past your front yard. During the time the Lamborn's lived there, passenger service had been discontinued on the Sacramento Northern, but there were still freight trains rumbling by that shook the house.

I only got to ride a SN passenger trains once. It was on an excursion train between Oakland and Pittsburg, held sometime during January 1957. The route between Oakland and Concord was about to be abandoned, and the Bay Area Electric Railroad Association chartered Holman built No. 1005 and the Salt Lake & Utah observation car No. 751 which is owned by the Bay Area Electric Railroad Association. I recall the day was rainy and miserable, but still turned out to be lots of fun.

The San Francisco & Napa Valley Railroad appears to have been a most interesting and rural interurban line. Its passenger service was terminated on September 12, 1937, at which time I was only nine years of age. Consequently, I certainly was not able to make it up to the Napa Valley on my own to photograph it. Electric freight operations came to an end at Mare Island during February 1942 at the request of the U.S. Navy. They claimed the overhead wires were interfering with their mobile loading cranes. The service was then dieselized.

I trust that you have enjoyed this two-volume series on the *Electric Railways Around San Francisco Bay.* Let us hear from you. We are talking about publishing a similar two-volume series on the *Electric Railways of Southern California.*

Donald Duke

December 15, 1999
San Marino, California

Twenty interurban-type cars were built in 1903 for Market Street Railway's heavy-duty line to San Mateo. The Laclede Car Company of St. Louis built cars No. 1225-1244 which were large, commodious, swift, and smooth riding. The Market Street Railway even rock-ballasted the private right-of-way portions of the 20-mile line. In this scene, photographed in 1935, car No. 1228 dashes along near Burlingame. — Ernie Leo - Donald Duke Collection

Market Street Railway

Over the years, San Francisco's public transit development has progressed from horsedrawn streetcars, to cable cars, to electrically propelled transit vehicles. At the turn-of-the-century, electric railways with overhead power lines had advanced to the point where they were the most popular mode of transportation. An electric interurban line was planned from San Francisco to San Mateo, more or less following Southern Pacific's commuter line to San Jose. The San Francisco & San Mateo Electric Railway was finally completed in December of 1902.

The United Railroads of San Francisco was formed March 20, 1902, as a consolidation of the San Francisco & San Mateo Electric Railway, the first Market Street Railway (horsecar, steam dummy, cable, and electric), the Sutter Street Railway (horsecar and cable car), and the Sutro Railroad (electric). After the consolidation took place, and a system organized, the 1906 earthquake and fire nearly destroyed it all. In the years following the disaster, the lines were completely rebuilt and some 500 new cars acquired. Then in 1906 and 1907 the system was beset with labor troubles. The revenue lost during the strikes, and the increase in wages caused the road's financial structure to nearly collapse. In 1919, a reorganization seemed mandatory, but it was two years before it took place.

The second Market Street Railway assumed control of the United Railroads of San Francisco in April 1921. The new company acquired control of 291 miles of street railway and nearly 600 cars representing many styles and vintages. Of the 291 miles of trackage acquired, 276 were electrically operated from overhead wire, and 15 miles were cable-operated railway. The new company carried on with no outward change.

In November 1925, control of the Market Street Railway passed to the Standard Light & Power Company. They appointed the Byllesby Engineering & Management Company to manage the railway. Under Byllesby the road began to improve. They purchased or rebuilt some 237 cars, modernized the car's power system, and changed to

Market Street Railway's San Mateo Line or the *40-Line* was in direct competition with Southern Pacific's commuter line between San Francisco and San Jose. The *40-Line* had two advantages, it was cheaper and it took passengers directly into downtown San Francisco, instead of the 3rd and Townsend station. (ABOVE) Car No. 1234 races down the right-of-way toward Burlingame and San Mateo with a light midday load. This scene was photographed on February 25, 1938. — Charles D. Savage (RIGHT) This large green and white sign was placed along the right-of-way at Burlingame, near the Southern Pacific station. It was photographed in 1939 when I was a kid. — Donald Duke

cushion seating which replaced wood slats or rattan seats. Quite a bit of track was replaced on the most heavily travelled lines. The fronts of each car were painted white for easy sight identification.

Several Market Street Railway franchises expired in 1929, routes which the Municipal Railway wished to take over. However, they had to purchase the tracks, even so it was a great loss to the company. One-man cars were introduced in 1934 on lines which did not operate on Market or Mission streets. It nearly cut the operating cost by one-third. As rails became surface bent and needed replacing, such lines were converted either to motor coach or trolley bus. On January 15, 1939, the Market Street Railway began to serve the new East Bay Terminal with streetcars and buses. Unable to pay for their share of new rail and paving, the Municipal Railway paid the bill and charged a monthly rental fee. More lines were converted to motor coach as rails became too rough, but the rails were not removed. As San Francisco became involved in World War II traffic, business was very brisk.

During the height of the war, the California State Railroad Commission castigated the Market Street Railway for its longtime neglect and mismanagement. As rolling stock came up for repair, it was sidetracked. The carrier continued to limp along. An election was held in the City and County of San Francisco to raise $7.5 million to buy the Market Street Railway. The vote was 102,640 "yes" and 85,000 "no." On September 29, 1944, the Market Street Railway became the property of the City and County of San Francisco. Many of the rail lines were in such horrible shape that they were quickly converted to motor coach after World War II. Of the Market Street Railway fleet of streetcars, only 170 cars were serviceable. The company was finally dissolved as of January 9, 1949.

Interurban car No. 1241 pauses at the Broadway station, just north of Burlingame, to pick up passengers bound for San Francisco's 5th and Market Street terminus. Southern Pacific's San Francisco-San Jose commuter line is behind the station. Unless you knew which direction a car was going, you had to watch the roller sign above the motorman's window. In this case he forgot to flip the dash sign to read "San Francisco." — DONALD DUKE COLLECTION
(LEFT) At San Mateo, the interurban cars looped around a block and came to rest, between runs, at 3rd and Railroad Avenue. — DON SHELBOURNE

The 12 "Big Subs" of the San Mateo Line were large and impressive interurban cars purchased after the San Francisco earthquake of April 18, 1906. They were built for the Philadelphia & Western Railway, who was unable to pay for them. The United Railroads of San Francisco picked up 12 cars for service between San Francisco and San Mateo. Albert Tolf, cartoonist for the *San Francisco News,* portrays a "Big Sub" en route to San Mateo. These cars drew a large amount of electricity and were slowly withdrawn from service. Tolf published all his cartoons in a book called *This was San Francisco.*— Courtesy Albert Tolf

Market Street Railway interurban car No.1244 rolls by the Mission-style Burlingame station of the Southern Pacific, while en route to San Francisco. Note the brick-lined girder rails in the street. They probably were laid when the line was built way back in 1903. Charles D. Savage took this classic photograph on October 10, 1938. When the Municipal Railway of San Francisco took over the *40-Line* on September 29, 1944, the big interurban cars were run through the shops and came out in Municipal blue and yellow bodies. (LEFT) Railroad fans always have to do something different, and in this case opted for a Type A car, No. 18, for a run to San Mateo and then a return to San Francisco. In this scene car No. 18 pauses alongside the San Mateo Southern Pacific station. — Donald Duke

Cars No. 1550-1749 were purchased, following the San Francisco earthquake in 1906-1907, from the St. Louis Car Company. This was the largest order ever made by the United Railroads of San Francisco. They were called the "Robertson-type" cars. Apparently they were considered smooth-riding for their time. In this scene, three "Robertson-type" cars are running up and down Market Street, circa 1910. — Donald Duke Collection

The Ferry Building, located at the foot of Market Street and the Embarcadero, is highly decorated for the Golden Gate International Exposition. Note the Key System sign which told of direct ferryboat service to the Exposition. In this scene, San Francisco Municipal Railway No. 114 loops around on the outside, while Market Street Railway No. 167 loops around on the inside. This is the position each carrier held on Market Street. Charles D. Savage took this interesting photograph on February 22, 1939. (BELOW) A 22-Line car works its way south and east toward 18th and 3rd streets (Central Basin Ship Terminal). This photograph was taken at Fillmore and Jackson in 1943, shortly before the Market Street Railway folded. — Harre W. Demoro

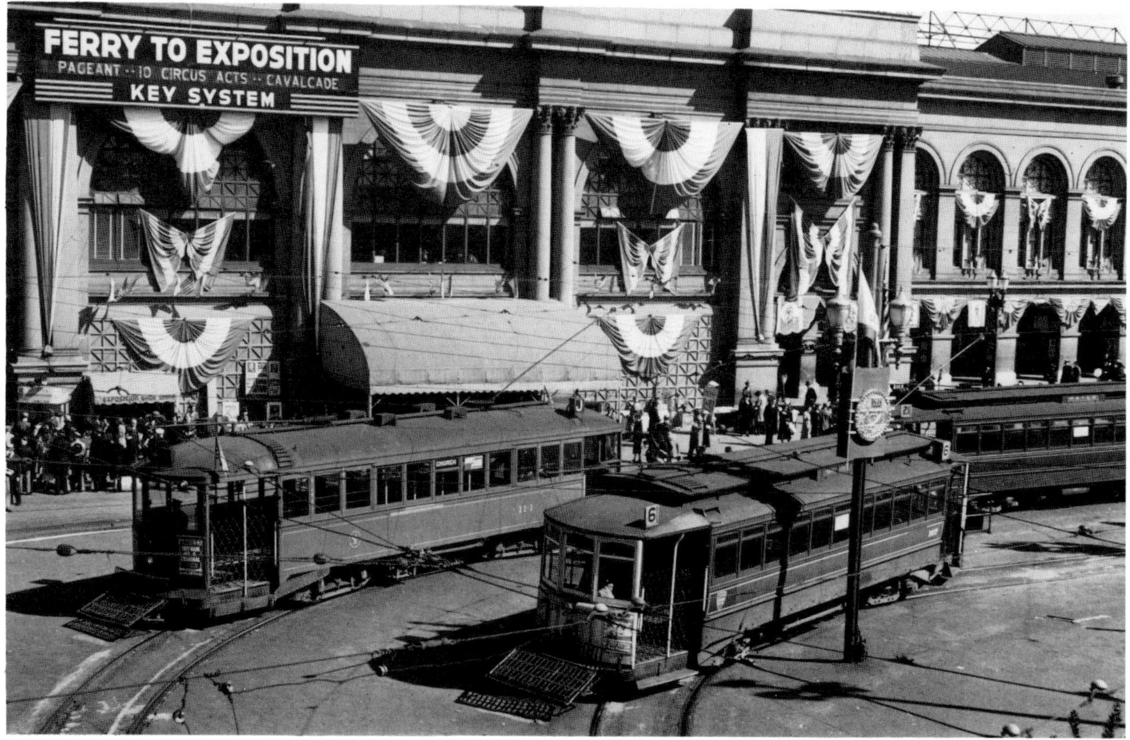

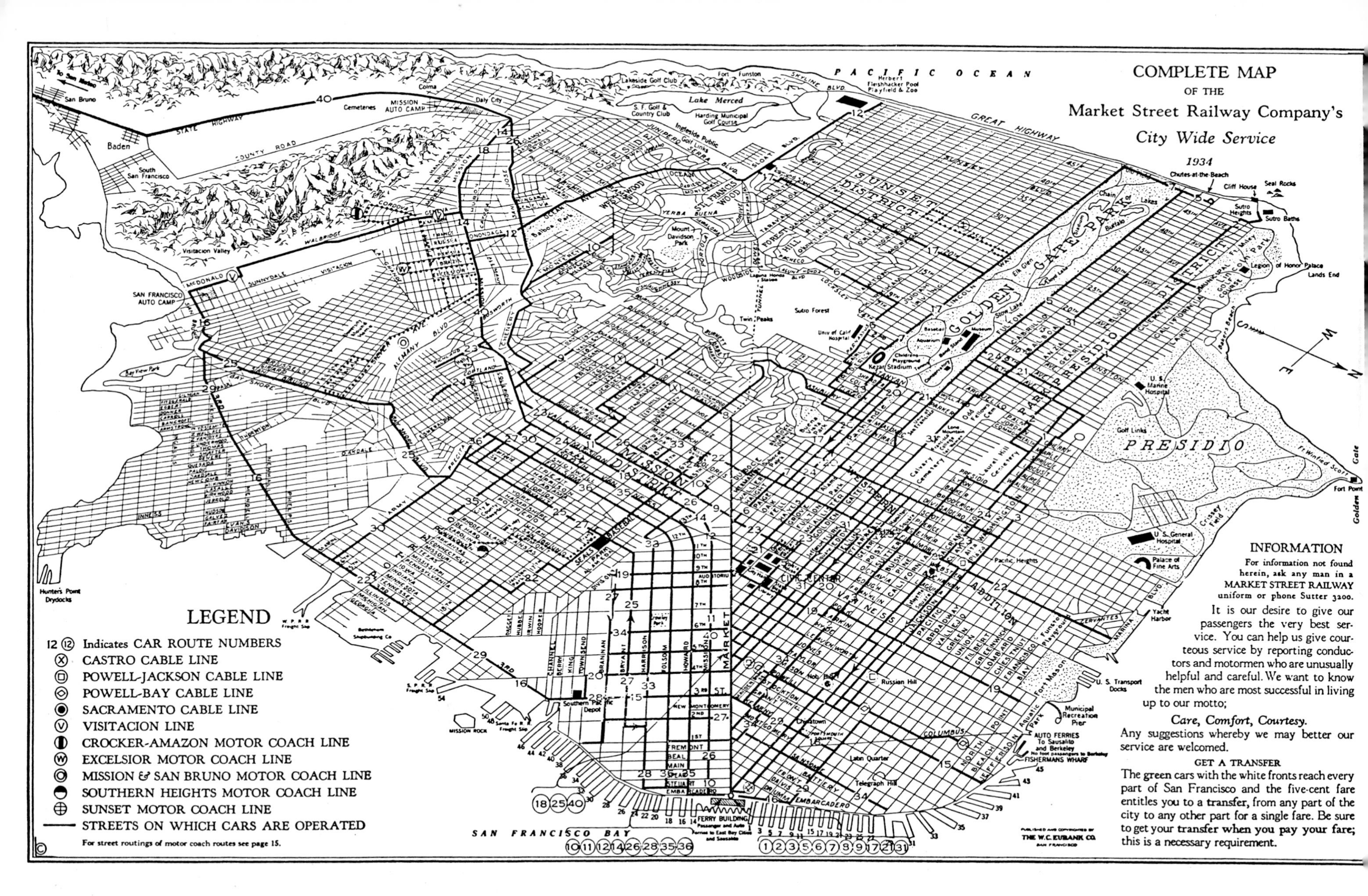

This map shows the city-wide system of streetcar and cable car lines operated by the Market Street Railway, as of 1934. I know this is pretty small and hard to read, but the dark lines are the White Front streetcar and cable car lines. This map was published in a tourist-style brochure of places to go and visit by streetcar. — DONALD DUKE COLLECTION

On September 13, 1941, the Northern California Railroad Club chartered car No. 1241 for a tour of the system. It was phographed at Polk and Broadway during a photo stop. — Donald Duke Collection

Car No. 248 waits near the Veterans Hospital for a scheduled run to return to the Ferry Building. This scene on the No. 1 Line is on Geary Boulevard on the west side of San Francisco. — Donald Duke Collection

Market Street Railway car No. 152 leaves Funston Yard en route to downtown San Francisco. — Donald Duke Collection

During World War II, Market Street Railway car No. 230 carried this sign on the side of the car. "Men and women wanted to back our fighters - Apply to be a motorman or conductor." — Jack C. Hammond

The No. 25 Line was restored to streetcars after previously been converted to motor bus just before the war. Car No. 868 is shown making the turn from Bryant to Army streets. This scene was photographed March 18, 1943. — Donald Duke Collection

Market Street Railway car No. 101 stops at the corner of 8th and Clement Street before returning to downtown San Francisco. — Arthur Lloyd

Car No. 944, on the No. 4 Line, loads passengers at Fulton and 6th Avenue for the return trip to Sutter Street in downtown San Francisco. — Donald Duke Collection

Car No. 278 rolls down San Jose Avenue in Daly City just before the end of the line. This car advertises to "Join the Coast Guard." — Donald Duke

Fillmore Street Counterbalance

The Fillmore Street Line was constructed in 1895 as a north-south streetcar line. Two blocks of this line, between Broadway and Green streets, were on a 24 percent grade. Too steep for a regular streetcar to navigate. So a cable counterbalance was installed on this line to raise and lower cars. Single truck cars were equipped with a gripping device, and cars were attached to the underground cable at both ends of the hill. The descending car counterbalanced an ascending car. The two cars passed each other at Vallejo Street. The Fillmore Hill counterbalance was discontinued on April 12, 1941. (RIGHT) Car No. 623 has made the crossover at the top of the hill, and a workman unhooks the cable. — Charles D. Savage (BOTTOM RIGHT) The two cars passing one another at Vallejo Street. — Harre W. Demoro Albert Tolf calls this the "Magic Rope Trick" in his cartoon book *This Was San Francisco.* — Courtesy Albert Tolf

Municipal Railway of San Francisco

San Francisco Municipal Railway car No. 1 rolls along Market Street, at Kearny Street, during October 1962 - the railways 50th anniversary. Car No. 1 was completely restored for the anniversary and is still used for excursions. During "Golden Week," passengers were carried along Market Street for a nickel fare. — Donald Duke

San Francisco's street railway system was mostly cable-operated before the 1906 earthquake and fire. Reconstruction followed the disaster, and replacement involved an entirely new electric streetcar system.

The story of the San Francisco Municipal Railway began before the turn of the century, when a new City and County Charter was passed in 1898, providing for a municipal street railway system. Money became tight, and nothing happened for several years. When the franchise for the Geary Street, Park & Ocean Railroad came up for renewal, the city saw an opportunity to start their system. Having all kinds of bond issues placed before the public, that were defeated, it was not until May 5, 1912, before bonds were passed, enabling them to buy the Geary Line.

The Geary Line was planned as a route from the ferries to the beaches. Mayor James (Sunny Jim) Rolph ran the first car on the People's Railway on December 28, 1912. The line did not reach its goal, as the Sutter Street streetcar line was operated with horse power on its eastern end (the city would not permit the United Railroads to electrify that portion of the line unless the private company allowed the MUNI to share its tracks). It was June 25, 1913, before it reached its goal. The Geary Line operated with 43 cars at the beginning.

On August 26, 1913, another bond issue passed by a clear majority, authorizing the eventual building of the C, D, E, F and J lines. With the Panama-Pacific International Exposition taking place in 1915, a line was run north on Van Ness, from Market Street, to the exposition grounds and the Palace of Fine Arts. Another line, the H-Line, was run out Potrero Avenue to the City and County Hospital. On December 29, 1914, the North Point F-Line opened. It ran out Stockton Street, and required a tunnel between Sutter and Sacramento streets.

The famous Church Street Line, with its run through Mission Park, and its serpentine trackage up the hill, was opened on August 11, 1917. There was a battle with the United Railroads about extending this line down Market Street from Church Street to Van Ness Avenue. It required

Dinky car No. 369 at the eastern terminal of the E-Line, in front of the Ferry Building. The E-Line covers the route of the old Presidio & Ferries cable car line. The car is painted brown, with a gray roof, and gold lettering. — DONALD DUKE COLLECTION

placing the J-line tracks outside of the United Railroad's tracks. This was the first use of four-tracks down Market Street.

Agitation for a tunnel under Twin Peaks began in 1908. For years it was just talked about. Finally the Twin Peaks Tunnel & Improvement Association was formed to open up the west side of the city. While the tunnel was under construction, real estate developers made a fortune selling lots on the peaks, and all the way to the beach. The tunnel was finally opened February 3, 1918, at the western end of Market Street. The courts finally granted the Municipal Railway the right to build down Market Street to the ferry terminal. Its tracks were on both sides of United Railroad's tracks, thus four tracks were laid all the way from the tunnel to the ferries.

During World War I, there was talk about buying all or part of the United Railroad's system since they were near bankruptcy. Some agreements had been reached, but talks eventually broke off. On February 16, 1921, the United Railroads was completely reorganized to save it. The outcome was the second Market Street Railway Company.

The Sunset Tunnel was excavated in 1926 to carry the Judah N-Line from Market Street to the beach. Mayor James (Sunny Jim) Rolph ran the first car through the bore on October 21, 1927. On January 9. 1932, jurisdiction over the San Francisco Municipal Railway was transferred from the Board of Public Works to the Public Utilities Commission of San Francisco.

Not much happened during the Depression except for the building of the loop track to the Transbay Terminal at First and Mission streets. Cars began operating to the terminal on January 15, 1939, picking up fares from passengers who rode the trains across the San Francisco-Oakland Bay bridge, which replaced an elaborate ferry system across San Francisco Bay.

Nearing bankruptcy, the Market Street Railway finally sold its system to the San Francisco Municipal Railway on September 29, 1944. With the sale, the MUNI inherited 440 streetcars, 38 cable cars, 9 trolley coaches, and 154 motor coaches. Most of the Market Street's streetcar lines were in such a horrible state, they were quickly converted to motor bus after World War II. In later years Market Street Railway's tracks on Market Street were replaced, and the MUNI outer tracks were removed.

Eventually the only streetcar lines remaining in San Francisco were: the J-Church Line, K-Ingleside Line, L-Taraval Line, the M-Oceanview Line, and the N-Judah Line. The main reason these lines have survived was because they used the tunnels or had very steep grades.

There was talk in the 1960's that the Bay Area Rapid Transit District had planned to build a subway under Market Street from the Bay to the Civic Center station, in order to reach Daly City. In the design it was planned that streetcars or possibly high-level rapid transit cars would use the first level of the subway and BART rapid transit trains would use the lower level.

With the MUNI Metro finally in operation, surface service on Market Street ended August 23, 1981. Starting in 1983, a trolley festival was held on the street tracks displaying historic and vintage trolley cars from Portugal, England, Italy, Germany, Australia, and the United States.

New standard Light Rail Vehicles (LRV) were ordered from Boeing-Vertol for service in the new subway, and to replace the venerable PCC streetcars. Muni Metro subway service was begun in phases from 1980 to 1982.

Since the Boeing cars were falling apart, a new fleet of LRV's, built by Breda, have been placed in service, replacing the Boeing LRV's. A new turnback facility has been installed and a new automated control system has been placed in the Metro subway.

Surface tracks were completely rebuilt from the Ferry Building to 17th Street. A loop was built at 17th and Castro, and tracks ran all the way to the Ferry Building. There was also the loop at the Transbay Terminal. The surface tracks on Market Street became the F-Line.

During January 1992, it was planned to build a line from the subway portal near the Ferry Building to the Caltrain Depot at 4th and Townsend. This line finally opened with a scenic ride along a private tree-lined right-of-way on January 10, 1998.

Construction is presently proceeding on a new E-Embarcadero Line which will provide service from the end of the subway and along the city's waterfront to Fisherman's Wharf. The line is schedule to be placed in operation in the year 2000.

In prewar days, Municipal Railway car No. 184 navigates the loop tracks at the Ferry Building, then heads for Chutes at the beach. Streetcar traffic was rather light on this Sunday afternoon. — ERNEST M. LEO

On June 7, 1942 the Northern California Railroad Club chartered "dinky" car No. 359 for a tour of the San Francisco Municipal Railway lines. The car was photographed at 33rd and California Street. — DICK JENEVEIN

After the merger on September 29, 1944, the MUNI took over Market Street Railway's Balboa (31-Line). They also painted out the white front of car No. 979. This scene looks east along Turk Street from Arguello Blvd. — HARRE W. DEMORO

Former Market Street Railway car No. 159 painted in post-merger livery, rolls down Market Street during replacement of the inside tracks. The No. 32-Line (Hayes/Oak) was later abandoned, circa 1948. — CHARLES D. SAVAGE

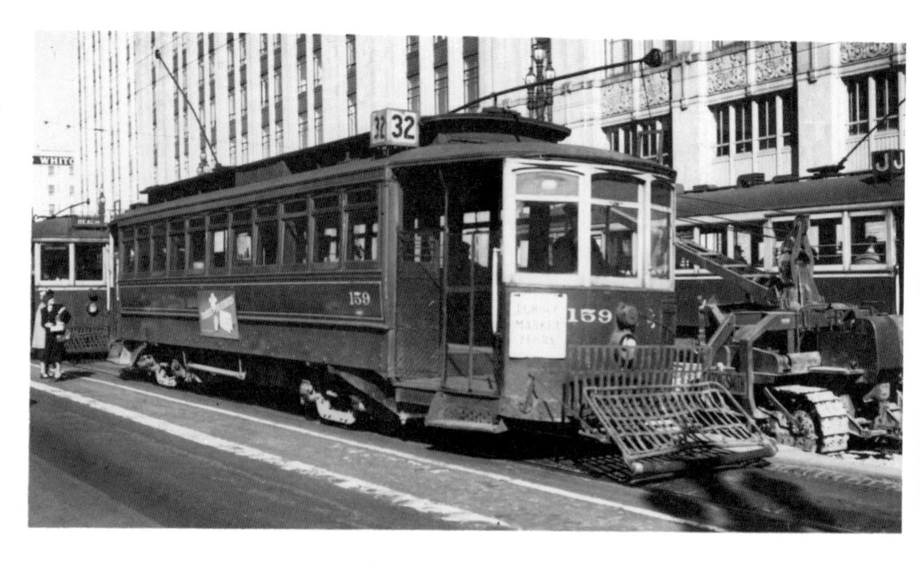

The motorman cautiously looks for traffic as he prepares to leave the 19th Avenue car stop on the M-Line. This car will eventually end up at Plymouth Avenue in the southern part of San Francisco. — George White

Trolley action on Geary Street as a C-Line car heads away from the Trans Bay Terminal on Mission, between First and Fremont Street. Note the five cars lined up behind car No. 116. — George White

Outbound car No. 94 climbs Geary Street, on what looks like a roller coaster track, between Divisadero Street and Presidio Avenue. This B-Line car is headed for the Cliff House and Seal Rocks. — George White

Car No. 106, running on the N-Line (Judah Street), turns off Market Street onto First Street. Then heads for the Trans Bay Terminal. — Harre W. Demoro

Under a light rain, car No. 25 exits the south portal of the Stockton Street tunnel located on the F-Line. The car is bound for Southern Pacific's Third and Townsend Street station. — William D. Middleton

A B-Line (Geary Street) car waits for its scheduled departure at Playland at the beach. Car No. 142 will round the Cabrillo Loop and head downtown to the Trans Bay "Bridge" Terminal, circa 1950. — George White

Car No. 916, complete with eclipse fender, rolls along Geary Street between Fillmore and Steiner streets. These fenders were done away with following World War II. — DONALD DUKE COLLECTION

Two cars, No. 202 and 174 layover at the end of the L-Line at 47th Avenue and Wawona Street. It is only a stones throw to Ocean Beach, circa 1951. — GEORGE WHITE

San Francisco Municipal Railway car No. 93 rolls east on First Street headed for the Trans Bay Terminal Loop. This B-Line car is coming from the beach and seal rocks. — GEORGE WHITE

Car No. 1, restored for the 1962 50th Anniversary of the San Francisco Municipal Railway, pauses for a picture stop during an excursion on Duboce Avenue. The United States Mint is located at the top of the hill, and No. 1 stands where the subway portal was constructed. The car is painted in the original gray paint, brick red roof, and gold lettering. — DONALD DUKE COLLECTION

An M-Line car rolls toward the downtown area after leaving its terminal at Plymouth. This photograph taken in 1950 shows construction along the right-of-way. — GEORGE WHITE

The motorman of an N-Line car, at the end of the line, strikes a pose for the camera. The scene is at the Great Highway turn around, circa 1951. — GEORGE WHITE

During the post-merger with the Market Street Railway, car No. 1225, operating on the San Mateo Line, rolls alongside Southern Pacific's Burlingame station. Just think of it, only 25 cents to ride all the way from San Francisco to San Mateo. This scene was photographed in April 1948, when just nine months later all service was ended on the 40-Line. — Charles D. Savage

Car No. 958 waits at the Ferry Building Terminal to take off on the former Market Street 14-Line which took it along Mission Street to Daly City. The car is apparently in its original colors, except for the white around the windows. The line ceased operations on January 15, 1946. — Harre W. Demoro

Market Street Railway's No. 9-Line was merged into the MUNI system on September 29, 1944. The 9-Line was called the Valencia Street Line. Inbound car No. 988 was photographed at Mission at 9th streets during January 1945. On November 25, 1945 the 9-Line was out of service. — Charles D. Savage

During 1951, when the Key System still ran trains across the San Francisco-Oakland Bay Bridge, San Francisco Municipal Railway car No. 200, off the M-Line pulls up to unload her passengers at the Bay Bridge Transit Terminal. Just ahead is an L-Line car loading up for another run to the beach. It is midday and traffic at the terminal is light. — George White
(RIGHT) This photographic postcard, purchased in the mid-1940's, shows MUNI No. 204, on the B-Line, complete with eclipse fender. — Donald Duke Collection

Two of San Francisco Municipal Railway's *Iron Monsters* pass one another at the west portal to the Twin Peaks Tunnel. It so happens that both cars are on the K-Line. Presently you can no longer see the fancy portal face, as this station has been covered by a roof. This picture was photographed during the 1950's. — George White

The San Francisco Municipal Railway had several car houses or barns. This is Presidio Car House. In this scene, an outbound B-Line car passes the car house en route to the beach. Three ladies are on the island waiting for the car. — George White

Car No. 183, on the K-Line, stops along Junipero Serra Blvd. to drop off three passengers. This car is en route to Brighton and Grafton Avenue, the end of the line, circa 1951. — George White

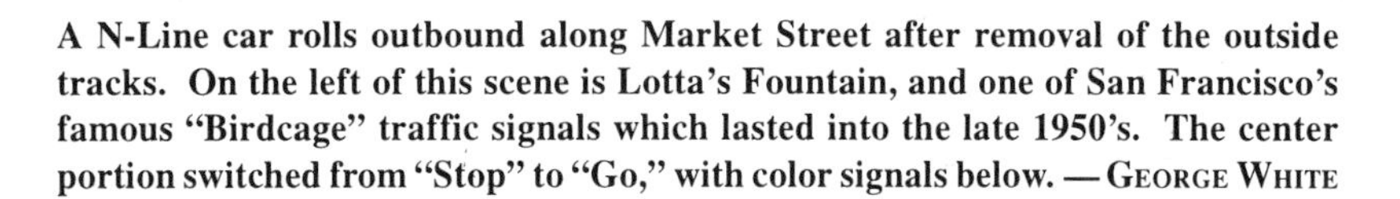

A N-Line car rolls outbound along Market Street after removal of the outside tracks. On the left of this scene is Lotta's Fountain, and one of San Francisco's famous "Birdcage" traffic signals which lasted into the late 1950's. The center portion switched from "Stop" to "Go," with color signals below. — George White

Magic Carpet car No. 1005 sits on one of the loop tracks at the Ferry Building. The five cars, delivered in 1939, were tested for comparison of motors, controls, and brakes. No more cars of this type were ordered. — J.C. HAMMOND

Magic Carpet Cars
No. 1001-1005

The Bay Area's first flirtation with streamlined streetcars came in 1939, with the purchase of five experimentally equipped cars from the St. Louis Car Company. Three cars had Clark B-2 trucks, and two had Brill 97-ER-1 trucks. Some had General Electric motors and controls, while others were Westinghouse equipped. Transit Research Corporation refused to allow the PCC label on the cars, so they were referred to as "Magic Carpet" cars. These cars were double-ended, with two doors on each side. The cars were delivered to the San Francisco Municipal Railway between July to November 1939. They were painted blue and gold. (BELOW) Magic Carpet car No. 1004 in green and cream livery, rolls outbound along Market Street near 8th, in 1948. Reconstruction of the center (Market Street) tracks and removal of the outer tracks (MUNI) is underway. — CHARLES D. SAVAGE

President's Conference Cars No. 1006-1015

The San Francisco Municipal Railway ordered ten double-ended PCC cars from the St. Louis Car Company in 1948. These cars were wired for multiple-unit control, but were delivered without couplers. Although the body shells were nearly identical with the prewar "Magic Carpet" cars, there were differences. They had a body cutout for easier access to the trucks, sloping windshield, and folding pairs of doors. The window arrangement was somewhat different and the front end was more protruded. (LEFT) No. 1013 at the end of the N-Line at Great Highway terminal, circa 1951. — GEORGE WHITE (BELOW) A side view of one of the new cars. When the MUNI went to a one-man operation, the rear doors were blocked with seats and window panels. — DONALD DUKE

Two PCC cars pass one another on rain slick Market Street at Duboce Avenue in the 1960's. If you look down Market Street, toward the Ferry Building, you will see a string of PCC cars. — Harre W. Demoro

Acquisition of a large fleet of PCC cars, and the abandonment of the Geary Street line on December 29, 1956, permitted the MUNI to retire the last of the two-man cars. Car No. 1040, the last PCC car to be constructed in North America, climbs the serpentine right-of-way of the J-Line. This car is about to enter Church Street from the private right-of-way at 21st Street. — Donald Duke

Trolley No. 1126 was purchased secondhand from the St. Louis Public Service Company. It is shown here loading and unloading at the Trans Bay "Bridge" Transit Terminal. — Harre W. Demoro

Rain clouds shroud Twin Peaks as the inbound PCC car, No. 1146, exits the east portal of the Twin Peaks Tunnel at Castro Street. This scene was photographed in 1969, just before the destruction of the portal. — Harre W. Demoro

Car No. 1162 rolls inbound along Taraval Street in the 1970's, bound for the Trans Bay Terminal. — Donald Duke (BELOW) Last days of the two-man "Iron Monsters" on Market Street was May 12, 1958. — George White

Light Rail Vehicles

A new term, *Light Rail Vehicle*, was introduced to San Franciscans during 1978-1979, with the arrival of 120 six-axle, articulated streetcars built by Boeing Vertol. Painted in the new MUNI colors of sunset red and California poppy gold, these new cars were very handsome. They were designed for both high-platform subway loading, and low-level street running. The cars were introduced at a leisurely pace due to all kinds of problems. It was not until February 18, 1981, that the N-Line (Judah) was converted to subway-surface operations with the new rolling stock.

Painted in the new MUNI colors of California poppy gold and sunset red, an outbound LRV, on the J-Line, exchanges private right-of-way for street running after ascending the serpentine trackage. — DONALD DUKE

A two-unit N-Line car, bound for the beach, is about to enter the Sunset Tunnel. (RIGHT) Two units roll along Duboce Avenue after exiting the trolley subway down Market Street. — BOTH DONALD DUKE

San Francisco Municipal Railway's Metro Subway was pristine when Light Rail Vehicle No. 1220 pulled into the Embarcadero Station on the opening day. Officials are gathered together for a ceremony on the inbound side of the station. — HARRE DEMORO

Kodachrome Cars on Market Street
The New F-Line

The new F-Line, stated to be the first streetcar line built in San Francisco in over 60 years, was approved in 1992. The F-Line involved the relaying of the tracks down Market Street from a loop at Castro and Markets streets, down Market to the Ferry Building, and then with a jog over to the Transbay Transit Terminal. Full service did not begin until September 1995 and operated with 15 PCC cars acquired in 1993 from the SEPTA in Philadelphia.

Each rebuilt PCC car was painted in the livery of a city which once operated this type of equipment on their streets. Surprisingly, the Market Street service was well received, and additional PCC cars are to be rebuilt.

Originally the F-Line was to run down Market Street to the Ferry Building, then the length of the Embarcadero to Fisherman's Wharf and the CalTrain depot.

The PCC cars running on Market Street are referred to as Kodachrome cars due to their multi-colors. These views were taken during an excursion as part of Sacramento's Railfair 1999.

Painted the colors of the Boston Metropolitan Transit Authority in an orange, cream trim, and silver roof, this car is about to take off for an outbound run on the F-Line. — Donald Duke

This car, painted in chrome and light yellow, is painted for the Los Angeles Railway, as it makes its outbound passage along Market Street. The car looks as modern today as the day it was purchased. — Donald Duke

While not on the F-Line, this PCC car is painted in the livery of the Red Arrow line of the Philadelphia suburbs. It has a maroon body color, off-white trim, and a black roof. — Donald Duke

Breda Light Rail Vehicles

Unlike the days of old, when a streetcar was built like a battleship and would last forever if maintained, as 1992 rolled around the Boeing Vertol Light Rail Vehicles were beginning to shake, rattle and roll. They were becoming very expensive to maintain. After months of planning, and evaluating bids, Breda Construzioni Ferroviari (Italy) was chosen to build 35 new articulated cars at a cost of $2 million each. If the U.S. Government was to pick up part of the tab, 50 percent of the work had to be performed in the United States and be from American parts.

The contract called for the first cars to be delivered by April 1994, and the balance by the end of 1995. Morrison Knudsen was to assemble the cars. Without ever testing a car, 17 additional cars were contracted for in 1994, and 84 more in 1995, making a total of 136 LRV's.

The first Breda LRV was due in May 1994, but was moved up to October due to clearance problems which had been overlooked on the original plans. The prototype car arrived January 12, 1995, and was rigorously tested. Four more cars had arrived by December 1995.

As the new cars began to arrive, they replaced the Boeing cars on the J-Line (Church) and other routes. Residents along the J-Line complained about the excessive whining of the LRV's and the vibration to their homes when the cars passed by. After a great amount of money was spent to try to solve the problem, little improvement developed, except to cut down on the noise.

Another 59 cars were ordered in July 1998, despite the noise and vibration problem. A paragraph in the new contract mitigated the noise and vibrations of the new units. At this writing, the San Francisco Municipal Railway operates its line with a mixed bag of new Breda cars, and Boeing Vertol cars that are still in good working order. Eventually all Boeing cars will be set aside.

An N-Line (Judah) train, consisting of three units, surfaces the MUNI Metro Subway at Folsom Street. It will then head south down the Embarcadero to the CalTrain depot at 4th and King streets. The new E-Line, when completed, will exit to the right and left of car No. 1421, and run between the CalTrain depot, the baseball stadium, and end up at Fisherman's Wharf. There is to be a junction with the F-Line (Market Street) in front of the Ferry Building. — Lowell Amrine

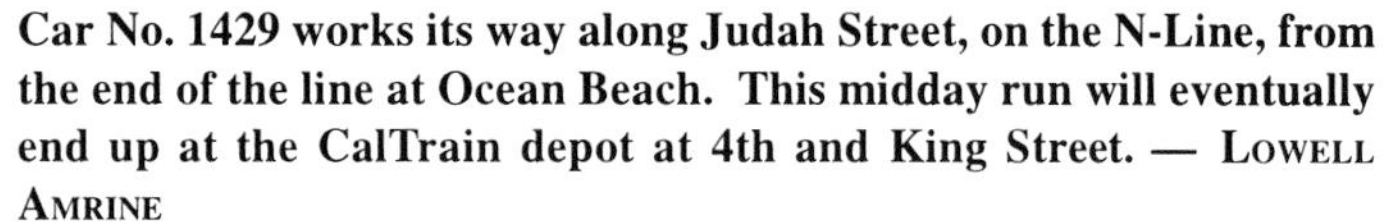

Car No. 1429 works its way along Judah Street, on the N-Line, from the end of the line at Ocean Beach. This midday run will eventually end up at the CalTrain depot at 4th and King Street. — LOWELL AMRINE

An Ocean Beach car stops at 46th Avenue and Judah Street, in the Sunset District, to let off riders. This scene is only a couple of blocks from the end of the line. — LOWELL AMRINE

Interior of one of the new Breda cars. This view shows how spacious these new cars are. Instead of the old-time straphangars, these cars have a pole at each seat to hang onto, along with a bar up high, running the length of the car. — LOWELL AMRINE

A N-Line inbound car pulls into the Embarcadero Terminal across the street from the CalTrain station located at Fourth and King streets. — Lowell Amrine

With the San Francisco-Oakland Bay bridge in the background, an outbound single-unit train leaves the Folsom Street Station for the MUNI Metro Subway. The next stop will be the Embarcadero subway station. — Lowell Amrine

A MUNI motorman waits for the signal to depart the CalTrain station. Upon entering the MUNI Metro Subway, he will surrender control of the trolley to a computer, leaving him to call the various stations and open and close doors. — Lowell Amrine

NORTHWESTERN PACIFIC
REDWOOD EMPIRE ROUTE
SAN RAFAEL
SAN ANSELMO
MILL VALLEY
SAUSALITO
TIBURON
RICHMOND
BOTHIN
ROYS
MANOR
FAIRFAX
PASTORI
LANSDALE
YOLANDA
HIGHLAND
BOLINAS AVE.
WEST END
B STREET
GOLF
CERROS
Tunnel 4
GLEN PARK
ROSS
KENTFIELD
CALIFORNIA PARK
Tunnel 3
GREEN-BRAE
ESCALLE
LARKSPUR
DETOUR
SAN QUENTIN
Prison
BALTIMORE PARK
CORTE MADERA
CHAPMAN
Tunnel 1
MEADOWSWEET
Tunnel 2
REED
ALTO
PARK AVE.
LOCUST AVE.
HIGH SCHOOL
ALMONTE
MANZANITA
WALDO
PINE
CANADA DE HERRERA
LAS GALLINAS
PUNTA DE QUENTIN
SAUSALITO
MARIN PENINSULA
TIBURON PENINSULA
RICHARDSON BAY
BELVEDERE
MUIR WOODS
Lake Lagunitas
Mt. Tamalpais 2604
SAN PEDRO PT.
SAN PABLO PT.
POTRERO SAN PABLO
RED ROCK
SAN FRANCISCO BAY
SOBRANTE
KRIEGER
GIANT
RICHMOND TRANSFER
A. T. AND S. F. RY.
STEGE
PT. RICHMOND
BROOKS I.
VIGORIT
NOBEL
FLEMING
UNIVERSITY AVE.
STOCK YARDS
PARAFFIN
SHELLMOUND
EMERYVILLE
RACCOON STRAIT
ANGEL I.
BLUNT PT.
N.W.P. Ferry
TENNESSEE COVE
Rodeo Lagoon
Fort Barry Military Res.
Fort Baker Military Res.
CAVALLO PT.
LIME PT.
PT. DIABLO
PT. BONITA
GOLDEN GATE
FORT PT.
ALCATRAZ I.
HYDE ST.
GOAT I.
KEY ROUTE PIER
OAKLAND PIER
WEST OAKLAND

Northwestern Pacific Railroad

One of the earliest rural electrification projects anywhere in the United States was carried out in Marin County, in 1903, by the narrow-gauge North Shore Railroad. John Martin, a pioneer in the development of electric generation, and his friend Eugene de Sabla, took over the control of the North Pacific Coast Railroad in 1902, and formed the North Shore Railroad. The narrow-gauge line ran some 80.93 miles between Sausalito, on San Francisco Bay, to Cazadero on the north California coast. At the time, many people were leaving San Francisco, moving across the bay into Marin County, to build upscale larger homes with surrounding property. Martin saw the potential for a lucrative commuter service with trains operated by electric power.

Martin decided on a standard gauge 600-volt overrunning third-rail system like the already proven systems in New York, Chicago, and Boston. General Electric motors and equipment would be used throughout the new line. Despite the road's steam railroad origin, the North Shore electrification was typical of the interurban practice throughout the country. Its wooden rolling stock was similar in size and arrangement to interurban cars of the period.

A standard gauge track, or another rail was laid between Sausalito, Mill Valley, San Anselmo and San Rafael. The main line between these points was also double-tracked, except for the Mill Valley line. An electric third-rail for electrical pickup was built between the two main line tracks, and the right-of-way fenced in to prevent citizens from coming in contact with the live third-rail. A new type of semaphore block signal system was installed to protect the main trains. Electric train service began August 20, 1903, between Sausalito and Mill Valley, and on October 17, 1903, to San Anselmo and San Rafael.

To initiate service, the North Shore ordered nine vestibule passenger-baggage cars, with one end of each car fully enclosed. They also ordered twelve vestibule coaches at the same time. The road rebuilt three open platform steam coaches into motorcars, and eight open platform

This General Electric photograph appeared in many trade and engineering journals about 1915 to show the electrification of railroads. Taken at Ross, this photograph shows the dual-gauge track and the rough wooden platform that covered the third rail in the station. Otherwise, the third rail was fully exposed out in the countryside. Combination car No. 352 has been equipped with an air-operated bell, and a Hedly anticlimber, the ribbed metal fitting under the door. This publicity shot is rather unusual because this photograph shows and eight-car train. — Duke-Middleton — General Electric Collection

steam coaches into trailer cars. The motorcars were equipped with two General Electric 66-motors and contained M-type multiple unit controls. Passengers were carried between Sausalito and the San Francisco Ferry Building by a fleet of four single-ended paddle-wheel steam vessels. Ferryboats also called at Tiburon to handle the steam-operated train service. The new electric cars would not win any award for speed. Top speed between stations was about 40-miles per hour.

The Atchison, Topeka & Santa Fe Railway obtained control over the North Shore Railroad in late 1904. The first thing they did was to standard gauge portions of the system. The Santa Fe had not made connection with their lines around Eureka, thus they sold a half interest in the railroad to the Southern Pacific in 1906. The Northwestern Pacific Railroad Company was formed in 1907 by absorbing all the little railroads in the area.

As business picked up, additional motorcars were ordered from the St. Louis Car Company, and more narrow-gauge coaches were converted into trailer cars. No further new wooden cars were acquired except for the conversion of old wooden coaches into trailer cars.

The railroad received its power supply at the standard direct-current rate of 550 volts from its new power plant at Alto, four miles north of Sausalito, and from a motor-generator substation at its San Rafael terminus. The Alto power plant received its three-phase current at 50,000 volts from the transmission line of the Bay Counties Power Company, later the Pacific Gas & Electric Company. The Alto plant transformed the voltage to 4,500 volts and reduced it to direct-current railway voltage by means of two motor-generator sets.

Since the Santa Fe Railway had no direct rail connection with its half of the Northwestern Pacific, except by tug-hauled car floats from San Francisco or Point Richmond, it decided to sell its half interest to the Southern Pacific in 1927. The Southern Pacific became the sole owner of Marin County's commuter electric railroad. Soon as the SP took control, the line would see its first new

With the pending abandonment of the Northwestern Pacific electric commuter lines, a railfan excursion was run on January 26, 1941, using cars No. 354, 327, and 330. The Railfan Special is all loaded, ready to go, as soon as the regular train (at the left) pulls away from the San Rafael station and steam locomotive No. 109 is attached. The excursion ended up on the Petaluma & Santa Rosa Railroad. — Charles D. Savage

passenger cars since 1909. Many of the old wooden motors had either been wrecked, destroyed by fire, or just fallen apart. In 1929, the Southern Pacific ordered five motorcars and five trailer cars from the St. Louis Car Company. The cars were anything but new in design, but had all the modern appliances. They were a near duplicate of Southern Pacific East Bay "Red Cars" ordered in 1911, for their Oakland, Alameda, and Berkeley service. The NWP cars were built from an aluminum alloy which made the cars quite a bit lighter, and they were carried on Baldwin M.C.B. motor trucks, with each motorcar powered by four 125 h.p. General Electric traction motors. The cars were austere just like the East Bay cars, however, did have an interior lining, and the 3-2 seating had upholstered seats. Another nine identical cars, divided between seven motorcars and two trailer cars were ordered from St. Louis Car Company in 1930.

Instead of being painted dark green like the wood-rolling stock, the new cars were painted in brilliant tangerine orange paint. The new cars also had porthole windows on each end, just like the East Bay cars. There was a sharp contrast between the new and the old equipment. The new cars were never painted again, and by 1939 the orange had faded to a patina of pink. The new cars were used in most regular service, the old wooden cars were brought out only as needed for morning and afternoon rush-hour service.

The completion of the Golden Gate bridge in 1937 afforded Marin County residents swifter automobile and bus alternatives to the electric train-ferry commuting. One could leave home by private automobile and be in San Francisco in half the time than by rail-and-ferry. Suffering severe losses, the Northwestern Pacific threw in the towel on its electric commuter service on February 28, 1941. With World War II coming on December 7, 1941, I am surprised that the California Railroad Commission did not direct the Northwestern Pacific to reopen its rail-ferry service, at least for the duration of the war.

Although passenger traffic dwindled in the later years, as highways drew passengers away from the electric trains, operations during the rush hours were generally heavy. In this view at San Anselmo, a Manor Branch train led by motor No. 302 rolls by Tower No. 4 and San Anselmo sub-station. (BELOW) A midday train rolls down the main line at Almonte, bound for Sausalito. Note that the baggage car is on the end of the train. — Both Charles D. Savage

On January 26, 1941, the Pacific Coast Chapter of the Railway & Locomotive Historical Society ran an excursion with steam locomotive No. 109 and wood electric cars No. 354, 327, and 330. Excursionists wait at San Rafael for an electric train to pass. — Charles D. Savage

A midday train off the Mill Valley Branch works its way down to the ferry terminal at Sausalito. A ferryboat may be seen at the right. — CHARLES D. SAVAGE

A train from Mill Valley approaches Tower No. 2 which controls trains entering the main line at Almonte. A train bound for San Francisco has let off a single passenger. The conductor pulls the signal cord to advise the motorman he can start the train. — CHARLES D. SAVAGE

A two-car trains, bound for Mill Valley, pulls into the little station at Locust Avenue. A single passenger waits on the bench. (RIGHT) Several evening commuters detrain at Park Avenue station on the Mill Valley line. The short Mill Valley Branch was single tracked. — BOTH CHARLES D. SAVAGE

The demise of the Mount Tamalpais & Muir Woods Railway in 1929, cut deeply into Mill Valley passenger traffic. As a result only commuters and a few hikers rode the trains. The beautiful depot became a bookstore on the abandonment of the line. — ART ALTER

Mill Valley Branch

A train off the Manor Branch rolls down the double-track main line at Chapman, circa 1938. — Charles D. Savage (RIGHT) Two of the most visible parts of the 1929-1930 modernization program were captured by railroad photographer Art Alter in 1938 at Baltimore Park. They were steel electric cars and the new Baltimore Park substation.

A Sausalito-bound train stops at Kentfield Station to pick up three ladies going to San Francisco to do a bit of shopping. Note the classic cars at the left, an early park and ride situation. — Charles D. Savage (LEFT) A San Francisco train pulls into Ross Station, just south of San Anselmo, to pick up four gents bound for the ferryboat connection. The most modern stations had the Northwestern Pacific oval emblem mounted on the wall. — Art Alter

Manor Branch

Tower No. 4 controlled the signals poking through the depot roof, and the switches which directed trains to Manor and San Rafael. The actual station is at the right, and a waiting shelter at the left. — Joe Moir

The junction at San Anselmo was quite compact. The two double-track lines from Manor and San Rafael merged here. The station, the tower, and the substation formed the hub of the city. In the above scene, a train bound for Manor pulls up to load waiting passengers. — Charles D. Savage (RIGHT) It was along the station's platform that trains from Manor and San Rafael - operating between Sausalito and San Anselmo as one train- were coupled and uncoupled here. Note the three trains in this scene. — Art Alter

San Anselmo

Tunnel No. 1, north of Alto, complicated operations. It was narrow, built on a curved approach, and visibility was limited on the south end even though protected by block signals. The siding on the right was for small tower cars used in tunnel maintenance. — Charles D. Savage (BELOW) A Sausalito-bound train has just cleared the tunnel and speeds to Alto. The sign reads, "1000 feet to tunnel signal - trains approach signal under control." — Art Alter

Tower No. 5, out of the picture at the left, governed movements through the junction of the cut-off and San Anselmo-San Rafael. In this view, the motorman has his hand on the controller, as his train leaves San Rafael for San Anselmo. — Charles D. Savage

At West End station in San Rafael, at the foot of G Street, an interurban train pulls into town from San Anselmo. This station was built in the late 1920's during a period of upgrading of the line. — Art Alter

San Rafael via San Anselmo

A wig-wag or automatic signalman protects a crossing near Manor as a 380-class steel train rolls downgrade, circa 1939. — CHARLES D. SAVAGE

Just south of Manor is Landsdale Station. In this scene, a Manor-bound train passes a lower quadrant semaphore signal at Landsdale and sets it to red. The Landsdale shelter and station stop is out of the photograph — CHARLES D. SAVAGE

Petaluma & Santa Rosa Electric Railroad

The residents of Sonoma County obtained interurban service with the formation of the Petaluma & Santa Rosa Electric Railroad in 1903. It was a consolidation of street railway lines in the two cities of its corporate name. The line also operated steamer service between San Francisco and Petaluma via Petaluma Creek, and then built the interurban line as a connection to it. The interurban line was placed in service between Petaluma and Sebastopol during October 1904, and was extended to Santa Rosa in December of that year. The line basically followed the rails of the Northwestern Pacific Railroad, who would not permit the P&SR to cross its rails until a court order was obtained. On July 15, 1905, the road was extended from Sebastopol to Forestville. Plans to extend south to San Rafael fell

One of four interurban cars built by the American Car Company for the P&SR in 1904. It was photographed by an unknown photographer in its chocolate brown paint scheme. Known by the crew who worked the cars as "windsplitters," these center-entrance cars were of rather unusual design. Each car carried a motorman, conductor, and a baggage-express handler. Although the cars had couplers, it is not known if they operated as multiple-units. These Class 51 cars each carried a name when new. Since the number is not visible the name remains unknown.

While Sebastopol was not in the center of the system, all trains between Petaluma and Santa Rosa, stopped at Sebastopol. The classic station sat in the middle of a large wye. In this scene, car No. 57 *Woodworth* has pulled alongside the station. — PHOTOGRAPHER UNKNOWN

through as the San Francisco earthquake destroyed many of the lines financial supporters.

During the 1920's, the Western Pacific wished to spread into the area of Sonoma County, and an attempt to buy the P&SR fell through. The Northwestern Pacific purchased the line in 1932 in an attempt to keep out all invaders.

The P&SR was planned as a passenger and freight line. Interurban cars were painted white at the start and then switched to yellow. By 1914, the interurbans were making 12 round trips daily between Petaluma and Sebastopol, and 19 round trips between Sebastopol and Santa Rosa. By 1916, the road fell on hard times and was reorganized as the Petaluma & Santa Rosa Railroad.

From the beginning, the P&SR had developed a strong freight business, and the farmers of Sonoma County supported the line. Petaluma being the egg capital of the world, found that poultry and produce shipped on the P&SR could be carried by freight, transferred to P&SR steamers, and bound for San Francisco overnight.

Passenger business fell sharply as automobile use developed, although there was no bus competition. The P&SR cut costs by making their interurban cars a one-man operation, but it was not enough. All passenger service was discontinued in 1932. The roads freight service continued to grow despite the lack of passenger income. With the development of the California Gravenstein apple production, it provided the road with a stream of refrigerator car business. Even during the Depression, the P&SR showed a good margin of profit. Freight was handled by a fleet of steeple-cab electric motors.

Overhead power was supplied by California Gas & Electric Corporation which fed the road's two substations at Petaluma and Sebastopol, which broke down the power to 600 volts DC.

Interurban car No. 51 *Petaluma* pauses in front of the Santa Rosa station in the middle of the street. Painted a deep yellow color because motorist could not tell the difference between a speeding interurban and the hundreds of white-colored chicken coops through the "Egg Basket of the World." — Tom Gray Collection

The Petaluma & Santa Rosa only assigned odd numbers to its passenger cars. It might appear this was done to show that the road's roster was bigger than it was. Car No. 67 was painted a chocolate brown color when delivered by Holman in 1904. — Tom Gray Collection

The Holman Car Company of San Francisco built six conventional interurban cars for the P&SR in 1904. They had end doors, with interior compartments for baggage-express, and non-smoking and smoking passenger. It is not known if the Holman cars were originally painted chocolate brown in color. — Tom Gray Collection

Homemade freight locomotive No. 10 is one of the original freight units at Sebastopol. It could be hauling rock during construction or debris from Santa Rosa after the Great Earthquake of April 18, 1906. — PHOTOGRAPHER UNKNOWN

After passenger service was discontinued in 1932, No. 55 was retained as an inspection car. It is shown here at Petaluma in 1941 without its trolley poles. It was eventually scrapped in 1943. — CHARLES D. SAVAGE

Electric locomotive No. 506 was photographed on a local freight. The location and the photographer are unknown. This engine was built in the company shops in 1923 from parts from former Sacramento Northern No. 1000 and the running gear and electrical parts from Ocean Shore No. 51. Note the unusual pantograph mount with the locomotive bell in the center.

Wood constructed electric locomotive No. 1004 was also a homemade unit, put together in the P&SR shops. It is said that the road built the body, the running gear and electrical parts were from an Ocean Shore locomotive. It was later rewired for multiple-unit operation. The locomotive was retired in 1946 and finally scrapped a year later. — PHOTOGRAPHER UNKNOWN

On April 6, 1941, the Pacific Coast Chapter of the Railway & Locomotive Historical Society ran an excursion over the lines of the Petaluma & Santa Rosa Railroad. The P&SR, lacking passenger rolling stock, ran the three electric cars and one main line car from the Northwestern Pacific. In the above view, the excursion train at Liberty making a photo stop. — Charles D. Savage

The excursion train returns to Sebastopol after the run north to Forestville. Passengers were not allowed out of the cars on the return trip. Note the Petaluma & Santa Rosa emblem above the front door to the depot. — Charles D. Savage

Northwestern Pacific electric rolling stock invades Sebastopol. Note the route sign on the rear of the passenger car. When the excursion train pulled into Sebastopol an army of railroad buffs invaded the station. — Charles D. Savage

P&SR No. 1008 as it appeared in 1938, out of service in the Petaluma yard. Note the fancy emblem on the side of the locomotive. Wonder what those steel cylinders are on the four corners of the engine? — Charles D. Savage

No. 57 was another passenger car saved from the scrapper when the P&SR discontinued passenger service in 1932. Charles D. Savage photographed her in 1939. Note the car still has its seats, however, the carbody has been steel sheathed, covering up the wooden sides. — Charles D. Savage

Photographer Charles D. Savage found No. 1008 switching a spur at Petaluma in 1946. This unit also appears to be a homemade electric locomotive.

Sacramento Northern Railway

It was a cloudy day on February 17, 1940, when Sacramento Northern's train No. 3 *The Meteor* pulled into the Bridge Terminal at 1:45 P.M., right on time. On this day the consist was cars No. 1003 and 1022. This train traveled some nine miles over Key System and bridge railway tracks, from the end of its line at 40th and Shafter in Oakland, to San Francisco. — CHARLES D. SAVAGE

The Sacramento Northern Railway was a high-speed interurban line stretching 185 miles from San Francisco through the Sacramento Valley, to the town of Chico. The railroad offered the longest inter urban ride in the United States, requiring a trip of little more than six hours. The Sacramento Northern was a merger of the Oakland, Antioch & Eastern Railway (San Francisco-Sacramento Railroad) with the Northern Electric Railway on June 20, 1918. The Sacramento Northern was eventually taken over by the Western Pacific Railroad as a freight feeder, but the SN retained its own identity.

In this pictorial presentation, we are only concerned with the southern end of the line as it relates to San Francisco Bay, or between San Francisco/Oakland, and the railroad car ferry at Mallard which crossed Suisun Bay.

The coming of the interurban made possible the short-cut crossing of the Coast Range. On account of the heavy grade required, the Southern Pacific chose to take the easy route by following the shoreline of San Francisco Bay, San Pablo Bay, and Suisun Bay. With electric power, the Sacramento Northern was able to make the run from Oakland to Suisun Bay in a much faster time, and over a shorter distance.

The Sacramento Northern's southern section was the idea and organization of five San Francisco capitalists. The portion of the line between Oakland and Sacramento was started by the Oakland & Antioch Railway, which was incorporated on January 13, 1909. The O&A began building from a connection with the Santa Fe Railway at Bay Point, and built west to Walnut Creek, by way of Concord. As the road built up Shepard's Canyon to where a 3,200-foot tunnel was being bored, the company fell on hard times.

The railroad was reorganized as the Oakland, Antioch & Eastern Railway on March 28, 1911. The long tunnel was completed, and rails were laid down the hill into Oakland. A terminal was established at 40th and Shafter streets in Oakland, alongside the Key System Piedmont Line (later C-Line) trackage. Rights were obtained from the Key System to run Oakland, Antioch & Eastern trains out onto the Key Pier Terminal. Here passengers were provided direct ferryboat service to San Francisco.

At West Pittsburg (Mallard), on Suisun Bay, the OA&E encountered its first water crossing on the run to Sacramento. Original plans called for a high bridge across the bay, and it had to be high enough to clear the masts of ocean-going vessels going upriver to Stockton. Such a bridge would be extremely expensive and would require approaches of nearly a mile in length on each side. In the meantime, a train ferry was placed in service between Mallard (south side) and Chipps (north side). From Chipps, it was nearly a straight shot on an even grade to Sacramento. OA&E trains reached Sacramento on September 3, 1913.

The distance from Oakland to Sacramento was nearly the same whether one took the Sacramento Northern or the Southern Pacific. Approximately 85 miles. The Sacramento Northern's crack trains *The Comet* and *Meteor* made the run from Oakland to Sacramento in three hours 15 minutes, including all stops. The *Overland Limited,* the Chicago-Oakland flyer of the Southern Pacific, making no stops, made the run in three hours and 40 minutes. This included the crossing of Suisun Bay by both trains which took about 20 minutes. Once the Southern Pacific erected its Martines-Benicia giant lift bridge in 1930, replacing the car ferry, it became a different ball game.

Unfortunately, the Sacramento Northern's profits were never as noticeable as its service, its speed, or the luxury of its interurban trains and parlor cars. The OA&E went into receivership and was reorganized as the San Francisco-Sacramento Railroad (the Sacramento Short Line). The Western Pacific Railroad, already in control of the Northern Electric Railroad, an interurban line running from Sacramento to Chico, had its eye on the Sacramento Short Line as a possible feeder railroad. It was also rumored that the WP was considering using the "Short Line" as a means of bringing in its trains to Oakland, thus saving many miles of running via Altamont Pass.

The San Francisco-Sacramento Railroad, the Northern Electric, and the Central California Traction Company built an interurban Union Station in Sacramento in 1926. The Traction Company was a joint venture operation of the Santa Fe, Southern Pacific, and Western Pacific. The Sacramento Short Line would have been abandoned if it had not merged with the third-rail Northern Electric Railway in 1928. Now all merged roads were under the control of the Western Pacific and became a giant feeder for carload freight hauled by electric locomotives.

The Oakland, Antioch & Eastern portion of the Sacramento Northern was built to the highest standard. Heavy overhead carrying the current, crushed rock ballasting the right-of-way, and its Holman-built interurban cars rode like Pullman cars. These interurban cars were 1,200 volt D.C. high-speed combination passenger-baggage cars operating between Oakland and Sacramento. Each car rode on Baldwin M.C.B. trucks and were powered by four Westinghouse traction motors of 140 h.p. each. The traction motors could operate on either 600 to 1,200 volts D.C. The electrical equipment was arranged to permit full speed operation on either the Sacramento Northern's 1,200 volt lines, or Key System's 600 volt lines. Each car carried one pantograph for operation on the Key System lines, or two trolley poles for current collection on the Sacramento Northern. Strange as it may seem, the Holman cars were painted orange prior to the OA&E-NE merger, and then painted Pullman green.

The opening day crowds were so large for the Oakland & Antioch Railway entrance into Oakland, that the interurban line rented day coaches from the Santa Fe Railway to handle the throng. In the above scene, O&A officials pose alongside car No. 1001, one of two cars built by the Holman Car Company of San Francisco in 1911. — Donald Duke Collection

Since the Key System was the major participant in the Bridge Railway across the San Francisco-Oakland Bay Bridge, the Sacramento Northern had to go along, or be left out in the cold and terminate its trains at 40th and Shafter. The SN began to use the rails of the San Francisco-Oakland Bay Bridge on January 15, 1939, at the same time as the Key System began service. Because Sacramento Northern trains ran so infrequently, few people remember the green trains on the bridge or at the San Francisco Terminal. The SN did, however, have a pretty good commuter business between Pittsburg, Concord, Walnut Creek, and downtown San Francisco. Actually, the heyday of intercity electric interurban service was nearly over by the time the Sacramento Northern decided to use the bridge rails.

When Southern Pacific's Interurban Electric announced on February 26, 1940, that it planned to throw in the towel and abandon all its East Bay commuter lines, the Sacramento Northern also went into action. The SN found this an appropriate time to end all of their San Francisco-Sacramento service. This happened on August 26, 1940. Their Pittsburg commuter runs lasted until June 30, 1941. However, two round trips ran on July 5 and July 12, 1941.

Carload freight service became very important to the Sacramento Northern, especially following the takeover by the Western Pacific. On the southern portion of the line, freight service was handled by two types of steeple-cab locomotives. General Electric B-B steeple-cab engines were of the 60-ton variety, with the body being manufactured by the American Locomotive Company. The other type were built by Baldwin-Westinghouse as B-B type steeple-cab units of the Class D design and weighing 65 tons. Electric freight service was provided on the southern end of the line until March 1, 1957, when it was abandoned between Oakland and Lafayette.

The Bay Area Electric Railroaders Association was able to squeeze in a last passenger run during January 1957 before the overhead wire was taken down and the rails removed. This final passenger run was a two-car train with interurban No. 1005 and former Salt Lake & Utah observation car No. 751.

The entrances to the tunnel were sealed with concrete and the freights were cut back to Walnut Creek in 1958. By 1964 the trackage between Walnut Creek and Concord was discontinued so as to allow the Bay Area Rapid Transit to build their test track.

The Oakland, Antioch & Eastern inaugurated first-class deluxe parlor car service between Oakland and Sacramento, almost from the start. For this service, the road acquired Henry E. Huntington's private car the *Alabama.* The car was rebuilt to provide a kitchen, pantry, and larger dining area. It never did have an open-end observation section. It is seen here crossing Lake Temescal on the train named *Meteor*. — DONALD DUKE COLLECTION

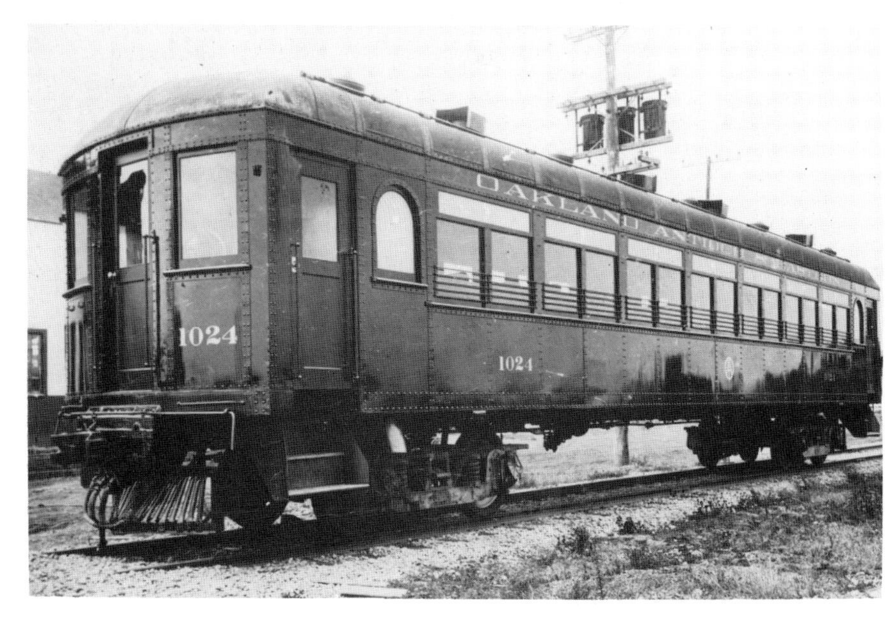

Eight all-steel passenger-car trailers were ordered by the OA&E in 1913 from the Hall Scott Motor Car Company of Berkeley. These cars proved to be the only all-steel passenger equipment ever owned by the road, or the Sacramento Northern. They carried the Nos. 1019-1926. — DONALD DUKE COLLECTION

When the Oakland, Antioch & Eastern arrived at Sacramento, its original depot was at the corner of Third and I streets. In this scene, No. 1010 and the parlor car *Moraga* wait for a return schedule to Oakland and San Francisco, circa 1914.

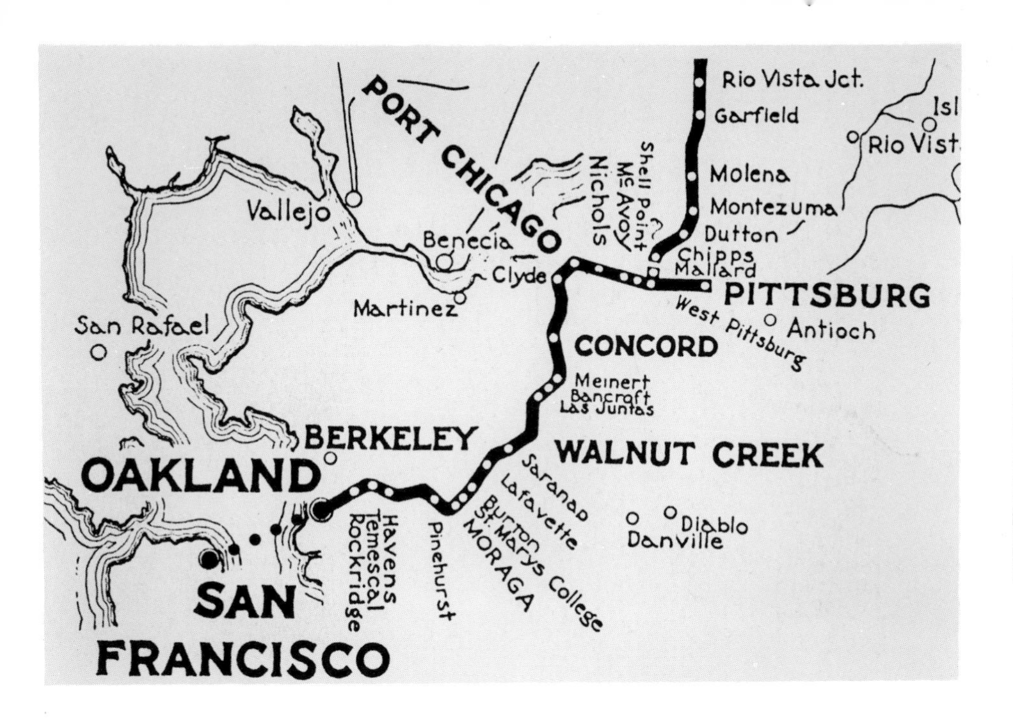

Train No. 3, *The Comet,* rolls down Shafter Avenue at Oakland on May 19, 1938, bound for the Key System pier terminal. This train consists of cars No. 1006, 1020, and the observation car *Sacramento*. During bridge operations, train No. 3 became *The Meteor*. — Charles D. Savage

Operating as the *Chico Passenger* on March 10, 1936, train No. 6, composed of cars No. 1005 and 1026, pulls into Oakland's 40th and Shafter station for an inspection before the long run to Chico. The curved building at the right housed the baggage room and trainmen's locker room on the first floor, and the accounting office upstairs. — Charles D. Savage

On Saturday September 23, 1938, Sacramento Northern No. 1015 arrived at 40th and Shafter after the long run from Sacramento. The Railway Express agent went right to work unloading the front end. At the left is the brand new Key System No. 127 temporarily connected with the Sacramento Northern prior to bridge railway service. — Charles D. Savage

Sacramento Northern crack passenger train, *The Meteor,* left the Key System pier at 5:18 P.M., bound for Sacramento. At 5:36 P.M. the train was photographed climbing the west side of the Oakland Hills at Rockridge Station Stop on August 10, 1938. A single passenger sits on the observation platform enjoying the scenery. — CHARLES D. SAVAGE

The Comet grinds up Shepard Canyon, near Pinehurst station, with the daily train No. 7 bound for the Key System pier, and the ferryboat ride to San Francisco. (RIGHT) No. 1004 pokes its head through the Havens Tunnel working westbound with train No. 29, the St. Marys to San Francisco passenger train. — BOTH CHARLES D. SAVAGE

Bound for Sacramento on Sunday only, train No. 18, *The Sacramento Passenger,* works its way eastward along Shafter Avenue in a strictly residental neighborhood. The train will swing onto Chabot Road and into the hills behind Oakland. — CHARLES D. SAVAGE

At 8:03 A.M. train No. 2 *The Comet* left the Key System pier for 40th and Shafter. It arrived at 8:24 A.M. and then headed toward Sacramento at 8:26 A.M. Charles D. Savage photographed the train just leaving 40th and Shafter with three cars and the observation car *Sacramento.* Note that the motorman forgot to put the train number in the indicator board.

En route from Sacramento, the *San Francisco Passenger* train No. 3, was photographed at speed near Valle Vista with a three-car train in 1938. It is fall, and the walnut trees along the right-of-way are without leaves. — Charles D. Savage

Sacramento Northern train No. 2, *The Comet*, left San Francisco at 7:40 A.M. en route to Chico. It arrived at Sacramento Union Station at 10:23 A.M. which will depart at 10:30 A.M. Baggage men load mail, express and parcels in the baggage compartment, while passengers relax in the cars. (RIGHT) Once the baggage and express is loaded, train No. 2 takes off from Sacramento Union Station for Chico. The train is scheduled to arrive there at 1:40 P.M. — BOTH CHARLES D. SAVAGE

Sacramento Union Station

The three electric lines operating out of Sacramento, the Central California Traction, the Sacramento Northern, and the San Francisco-Sacramento, completed a Union Station on H Street during the Fall of 1926. Prior to the Union Station, each railroad had their own station, requiring passengers and luggage to transfer from one station to another, thus causing delays. The Union Station was located in the center of the hotel and shopping district of Sacramento. Passenger loading was at the rear of the station, with tracks circling in from 11th and 12th streets. At the end of passenger service, the area became a supermarket.

The contrast between Sacramento Northern's rolling stock from the former Northern Electric and the Oakland, Antioch & Eastern. No. 129 is a former NE car built by the Niles Car & Manufacturing Company on Woodland train No. 42. The No. 1015 is a former Holman Car Company product originally purchased by the OA&E. The No. 1015 will be bound for San Francisco. These two cars were photographed at the Sacramento Union Station on May 19, 1940. — CHARLES D. SAVAGE

Sacramento Northern's train *The Meteor* works its way through the bridge yards on January 15, 1939, bound for the San Francisco-Oakland Bay bridge and San Francisco. Four big, high-speed cars, were built by Holman in 1912, numbered 1003-1006. In 1913 additional copycats were built by the Cincinnati Car Company and Wason Car Company as Nos. 1007-1017. — Charles D. Savage

Interurban car No. 1006 ran as a test car preceding the start of Sacramento Northern operations over the San Francisco-Oakland Bay bridge in 1939. — Charles D. Savage

As passenger traffic began to slow down over the years, the Sacramento Northern depended heavily on a sizeable amount of freight traffic. After the end of passenger service, the Sacramento Northern maintained its electric freight business. In this scene, with electric locomotive No. 661 on the headend, leaves 40th and Shafter for Sacramento on June 21, 1944. This freight had an electric pusher on the rear to surmount the grade out of Oakland. — Charles D. Savage

Freight

Photographed during World War II, locomotives No. 603 and 604 work by Terrace Station Stop and move toward Havens, and the tunnel under the Oakland Hills. When photographed June 3, 1944, the locomotives still had their long hoods over their headlights. — Charles D. Savage

Electric locomotive No. 604 waits for a freight assignment at the 40th and Shafter Avenue yard in 1936. Built by the Baldwin-Westinghouse combination in 1912 for the Oakland, Antioch & Eastern, it kept its same number on the Sacramento Northern. — Charles D. Savage

The Bay Area Electric Railroad Association was able to squeeze in a final passenger run over the southern section of the Sacramento Northern during January 1957. On the trip between Oakland and Mallard, a photo stop was made at the east portal of the Havens Tunnel. Several railfans got off, the train backed inside, then slowly came forward for this very last photograph. Note the throng of railfans in the motorman's compartment. — DONALD DUKE

How would you like to have this long freight train running up your residential street? Well that is what you got on Shafter Avenue in Oakland. In this scene taken during the last days of electric freight service, No. 606 pushes and No. 604 pulls as this freight makes it up Shafter Avenue. — Donald Duke

End of the Line

The Sacramento Northern abandoned their electric freight operations between 40th and Shafter, and Lafayette, on March 1, 1957. A connection was made in Oakland so the Western Pacific could interchange with the Oakland Terminal Railway. Service between West Lafayette and Pittsburg was later converted to diesel. On August 10, 1958, the trackage between Lafayette and Walnut Creek was abandoned, and then later to Concord in order to provide the Bay Area Rapid Transit its test track.

The Walnut Creek station looks quite forlorn in this 1957 scene. No. 145 has just brought in a couple of freight cars. The catenary has been taken down, but the support wires are still up. This trackage became the Bay Area Rapid Transit test track. The BART Walnut Creek station now sits on this site. — Harre Demoro

Would you believe this was Moraga? Today it is a sea of homes and structures. When the Sacramento Northern abandoned the rails into Oakland, trains still operated on the eastside. Here a short westbound freight works its way from Pittsburg. Moraga can still be read over the boarded-up station building at the left. — Donald Duke

THE VALLEY OF THE GEYSERS
NAPA
ST. HELENA
CALISTOGA
ELECTRIC ROUTE
MIDDLETOWN
MT. ST. HELENA
ÆTNA SPRINGS
POPE VALLEY
MONTICELLO
CALISTOGA
ANGWIN
CHILES VALLEY
ST HELENA
SANITARIUM
WHITE SULPHUR SPRINGS
BELLO
RUTHERFORD
OAKVILLE
VETERANS HOME
YOUNTVILLE
SANTA ROSA
SAN FRANCISCO, NAPA & CALISTOGA ELECTRIC R.R.
TRUBODY
DARMS
OAK KNOLL
NAPA SODA SPRINGS
SONOMA
NAPA
NAPA STATE HOSPITAL
SUSCOL
NAPA JUNCTION
ST JOHN'S MINE
PETALUMA
FLOSDEN
SULPHUR SPRINGS
VALLEJO
NAPA BAY
MARE ISLAND
NAVY YARD
PORT COSTA FLOUR MILLS
DAVISVILLE
ELECTRIC LINE
VACAVILLE
FAIRFIELD
SUISUN
ROCKVILLE
CORDELIA
CRESTON
PROPOSED
SAN PABLO BAY
MONTICELLO STEAMSHIP CO.
CARQUINEZ
SELBY SMELTING WORKS
POINT PINOLE
SAN RAFAEL
POINT SAN PEDRO
POINT SAN PABLO
WINEHAVEN
SAN QUENTIN
GEYSERS

San Francisco, Napa & Calistoga Railroad

This interurban car was built for the Vallejo, Benicia & Napa Valley Railroad in 1905 by the American Car Company of St. Louis. Your author found this photograph in the Library of Congress as part of a copyrighted illustration showing an auto stage service between St. Helena to Lake County points. The postcard stated the first run of the auto stage was May 19, 1908, and the electric cars run to San Francisco seven times daily. — Library of Congress

At the turn of the century, a traveler desiring to journey north from the San Francisco Bay, to the Napa Valley wine country, had available to him what was the ultimate transportation system. Part steamer and part interurban. He would board a Monticello steamer at the Ferry Building in San Francisco, ride 30 miles across San Francisco Bay, and at Vallejo board an interurban train for a swift ride north through California's richest valley - the majestic Napa Valley.

The reliability of this joint ship-rail service did much to develop the Napa Valley before the motor truck replaced rail freight. The San Francisco & Napa Valley Railway was built at the height of the interurban era, and extended north from Vallejo to Calistoga, a distance of 43 miles. The road was primarily a passenger line. It was unable to develop enough freight traffic to enable it to continue beyond the 1930's. That is except for the great amount of switching for Vallejo's Mare Island Naval Yard.

During its lifetime, the road operated under several different names. Initially, it was the Vallejo, Benicia & Napa Valley Railroad. On June 4, 1906, it was reorganized as the San Francisco, Vallejo & Napa Valley Railroad, and then in November 1911 became the San Francisco, Napa & Calistoga Railway. The line reached Napa from Vallejo on July 4, 1905, to Yountsville on August 23, 1907, to St. Helena on January 1, 1908, and finally to Calistoga on September 2, 1908.

Service was generally at two-hour intervals dictated largely by the Monticello ship schedules. The road was built as an experimental Westinghouse alternating current line. Cars ran on 750 volts A.C. and were heavy 60-ton interurban cars built by the American Car Company and the Niles Car & Manufacturing Company. Later two steel cars were acquired from the Visalia Electric. Trains consisting of two-cars were the general rule. One a Railway Post Office car and the other a coach. The Napa Route carried all the mail for the Napa Valley. Passenger traffic was rather heavy, due to the thickly settled communities of fruit and vegetables ranches. For years, even after the coming of the private automobile, the railroad offered the fastest service because of the lack of more than two lane highways. Hence motor bus competition almost did not exist. Also rival Southern Pacific only offered two trains per day up and down the Napa Valley, but they stole all the freight business and offered connections across the country. The depression caused a one-half drop in both passenger and freight traffic. In 1932, a huge fire destroyed the carbarn at Napa, and most of the passenger rolling stock. It also put their power plant out of service.

To replace the fire lost cars, two heavy steel cars were ordered from the St. Louis Car Company in 1933. These cars, the last interurban cars built in America, were placed in service on July 1, 1933. For the next four years the road was only able to offer three round trip schedules a day. The company went into receivership in 1934, and reorganized as the San Francisco & Napa Valley Railroad. The final blow came when on September 12, 1937, the ferry service to San Francisco was discontinued. Without a connection to San Francisco, the interurban line could not survive. The last passenger train was run September 20, 1937.

The railroad north of Napa was discontinued and the rails and overhead removed. The line from Vallejo to Napa received the same fate in 1942. The lucrative Mare Island switching service and freight line was dieselized and continued until 1957. That year the U.S. Navy took over the company and the switching service.

With the completion of the extension to St. Helena, the railroad was renamed the San Francisco, Vallejo & Napa Valley Railroad Company. Eight additional interurban cars were acquired, and one box motor, from the Niles Car & Manufacturing Company. In the view above, interurban car No. 42 will run as train No. 7 between Napa and the Monticello Steamship Company wharf at Vallejo on Napa Bay. In the background is steel car No. 61 and Niles car No. 40. (RIGHT) Interurban cars No. 46 and 52 wait on the ready track at the Napa depot, circa 1937, for a run to Vallejo wharf. The general offices of the railroad were on the second floor of the Napa depot. — BOTH CHARLES D. SAVAGE

Combination car No. 42 has just arrived at Napa as train No. 6 from the Vallejo wharf. She has unloaded her passengers, and patiently waits in front of the station and general office building. The Southern Pacific freight house may be seen in the background. — Charles D. Savage

Bound for Calistoga, a two-car train leaves Napa and shortly thereafter crosses over Milliken Creek. This train is powered by steel car No. 62, built by the St. Louis Car Company in 1932, and is shown here hauling trailer car No. 53, built by Niles Car Company in 1913. — Charles D. Savage

In 1927 the Monticello Steamship Company sold out to the Golden Gate Ferry Company, who in turn merged with Southern Pacific in 1929 to become the Southern Pacific Golden Gate Ferries, Ltd. Napa Valley Route No. 42 and Railway Post Office-Railway Express car No. 56 wait for the 7:30 A.M. ferry out of San Francisco, with arrival at Vallejo wharf at 9:20 A.M. The interurban train would arrive at Calistoga at 11:08 A.M. This view was taken March 6, 1936. — Charles D. Savage

The bellweather of Napa Valley Route's freight fleet was box motor No. 100. It is shown in this scene along California State Route 12 south of Napa with Napa Route's own freight cars No. 512, 519, and 507. Note the volume of traffic in this March 1937 scene. — Charles D. Savage

Calistoga-bound train No. 4 is not well patronized in this 1937 scene at Vallejo wharf. The Southern Pacific Golden Gate Ferries, Ltd. schedule is painted on the wall of the dock. — Charles D. Savage (RIGHT) Combination cars No. 62 and 63 are parked alongside the Napa carhouse in 1937. — Richard H. Young

Commercial photographer M.H. Strong of Napa was commissioned to photograph the two new high-speed interurban cars, sitting alongside an orchard, which arrived in May 1933. With Westinghouse 132-A motors, these two cars became the stalwart of interurban service between Vallejo wharf and Calistoga. These steel combination cars were ordered from St. Louis Car Company in 1932. — Duke-Middleton Collection

Napa Valley Route's train No. 9 left Calistoga for the Vallejo wharf at 1:25 P.M., and was photographed at speed near Rutherford, south of St. Helena, at 1:53 P.M. on July 4, 1937. Looking in the windows, it would appear that the interurban was nearly empty. (MIDDLE LEFT) Car No. 63 rolls along at speed as it enters the outskirts of Vallejo on the same day. — BOTH CHARLES D. SAVAGE

During the waning days of the Napa Valley Route, an all-steel train rolls through the Matt flag stop en route to St. Helena and Calistoga, on the northern end of the line. In this view No. 60 leads the train, followed by cars No. 62 and 56. Car No. 60 came from the Visalia Electric. — CHARLES D. SAVAGE

Railroad photographer Charles D. Savage photographed this meet at Oakville, between Yountville and Rutherford, on July 4, 1937. Interurban No. 62, operating as train No. 5 bound for Vallejo wharf and San Francisco, waits on the siding for train No. 6 bound for Calistoga. Train No. 6 was running nearly 20 minutes late. As a single-track railroad, it was a must that trains meet at passing sidings.

Mare Island Freight Line

Shortly after the turn of the century, Baldwin-Westinghouse produced a number of distinctive box-cab electric locomotives for several of their interurban customers. The San Francisco, Napa & Calistoga liked the design, but lacked the funds to buy a new engine out of the catalog. In 1922, they built a 60-ton box cab look-alike at their Napa shops. While the frame and car body were homemade, the locomotive was equipped with Baldwin 84-30A M.C.B. trucks and fitted with four Westinghouse 100 h.p. motors.

Mare Island is actually not an island at all, but is part of a peninsula separated by Dutchman Slough. Mare Island is separated from Vallejo by the Napa River. The Mare Island Navy Yard was established by Congress on August 31, 1852, and freight service was provided by the Napa Valley Route with the construction of a causeway in 1920. Little did the railroad realize that this short shuttle would eventually be the savior of the railroad.

The function of the Mare Island Navy Yard was to maintain and repair all Navy vessels, mostly destroyers and submarines. The Yard did employ some 5,000 workers. Along San Pablo Bay are giant cranes, drydocks, shipbuilding ways, warehouses, and a Naval hospital. The Napa Valley Route was its only railroad connection. Old No. 99 carried the name "Mare Island Freight Line" from early times, then named "Navy Yard Freight." The line was converted to diesel motive power when it was found that the overhead wire interferred with giant cranes installed during World War II. The overhead was taken down and No. 99 retired. (ABOVE) The Mare Island Freight Line with four carloads of freight at Napa Junction in 1941. — Will Whittaker

One can't help but wonder what someone might have thought when they saw a string of antique elevated cars coming down the line to Richmond painted in battleship gray. In 1942, the United States Maritime Commission was desperate for rolling stock, and these elevated cars were all they could muster. In this scene, a six-car Shipyard Railway train, bound for Richmond shipyards, rolls through the southern limits of Richmond, California, on April 1, 1944. — CHARLES D. SAVAGE

Shipyard Railway

When the Japanese attacked Pearl Harbor, Hawaii, December 7, 1941, the railroads of the San Francisco Bay area were totally unprepared to meet the emergency. All of a sudden the East Bay became an important war production center and the West Coast shipping point. With the establishment of additional war production plants and quick build up of the Richmond shipyards, the task of transporting the additional thousands of workers to their jobs also became a big problem.

The discontinuance of Sacramento Northern service and the total abandonment of the "Big Red Cars" of the Interurban Electric Railway left a huge hole in the public transportation system. However, most of the defense industries and installations in Oakland and Berkeley were close to Key System's rail and bus lines. With most of Interurban Electric's facilities still in place, except for those lines taken over by the Key System, it is small wonder that the California Railroad Commission did not restore service, at least for the duration of the war.

Industrialist Henry J. Kaiser greatly enlarged his shipyards at Richmond. At the time these shipyards were situated in a remote location from the metropolitan area, and also some distance from local transit service since the abandonment of the East Shore & Suburban Railway. Prior to the war, Henry J. Kaiser had contracted for 30 Liberty ships with the government of Britain, and now he had contracts for many Victory ships from the United States government.

Various proposals were studied. They resulted in the construction of a new electric line to be under the direction of the United States Maritime Commission. One plan was for an electric locomotive drawn train to be hauled over sections of the Key System, the abandoned Interurban Electric, and a portion of the Southern Pacific. But, of course, the Southern Pacific said "no." Gasoline and tire rationing soon limited the use of the private automobile.

On June 6, 1942, the Maritime Commission announced that an agreement had been reached with the Key System to construct and operate, under contract, a new railway from the end of its No. 2 streetcar line on San Pablo Avenue to Richmond. New materials were out of the question, so it became necessary to scour the area for rail, ties, overhead wire, substations, etc. It was no easy task. Rails were taken from every unused siding, from the abandoned Interurban Electric lines not taken over by the Key System, and from the former San Francisco & Napa Valley Railroad. Overhead wire was obtained from abandoned Interurban Electric trackage, the Bridge Railway, and the abandoned Key System streetcar lines. A search also went out for rolling stock to operate on the line. Why the former Interurban Electric or Northwestern Pacific cars were not used remains a mystery.

A front page story appeared in the *Oakland Tribune* for June 19, 1942. It announced that some 90 odd, wooden, elevated cars had been acquired from New York's Interborough Rapid Transit. During August 1942, the cars were processed through the Key System's Emeryville Shops on a 24-hour basis. The cars were repaired, scrubbed, painted battleship gray, had pilots installed on both ends of the cars, wired for headlights, and pantographs for current collection bolted to the roof of each two-car unit. The Shipyard Railway was scheduled to begin operation on December 1, 1942, but it was January 18, 1943, before things began to roll.

If ever a railroad was old, and half a century out of date the day it opened, it was the Shipyard Railway. Everything was secondhand and worn out. The line had two terminals, one at 40th and San Pablo, where connections could be made with Key System transbay trains, several streetcar lines and bus routes. The other was just over the Emeryville boundary, at the foot of Louise Street.

The Shipyard Railway ran north out San Pablo Avenue, using the tracks of the Key System No. 2 streetcar line. It then switched over to Ninth Street on former IER trackage to its end, then crossed the main line of the Southern Pacific on a large wooden trestle. Most of its timber had been salvaged from the abandoned Key Route pier. After crossing the SP, the line ran out Potrero Avenue to Kaiser Shipyard No. 1, and No. 3, then later to No. 3-A.

Operation was by timetable, and most of the runs coincided with the shift changes at the shipyard which operated around-the-clock. The old elevated cars were small, hardly larger than a streetcar, so, consequently, were run in long trains. The cars had no steps or anyplace to put steps without completely rebuilding, so loading platforms had to be constructed at each station or passenger stop. Although the trains ran full at shift changes, the Shipyard Railway operated at about 20 percent of capacity.

Riding the line was like an adventure into the 19th century. The wooden cars were loose and the joints moved back and forth when the cars ran about 40 miles per hour. The air brakes were turn-of-the-century and when they grabbed, it made the ride very jerky. It was hard on standing passengers who had to hang onto the straphangers for dear life. The rattan seats were hard as a rock, making them very uncomfortable on the derriere.

The war in the Pacific ended on August 15, 1945, but the shipyards continued building ships. However, when gasoline rationing ended, shipyard workers quit riding the trains. The Key System was then offered the line, but it would have required complete rehabilitation plus relocating the line to downtown Richmond. Service was suspended on September 30, 1945, and the railway was dismantled soon afterwards.

FROM RICHMOND SHIPYARDS

Key System — April 23, 1944

Leave Yard No. 3	Leave Yard No. 4	Leave Yard No. 1	Leave Yard No. 2 (14th & Potrero)	Leave Buchanan St.	Leave University Ave.	Leave Ashby Ave.	Arrive 40th & San Pablo
		6.15w	6.19w	6.32w	6.37w	6.42w	6.47w
			*6.50w	7.07w	7.12w	7.19w	7.25w
			*7.15w				7.45w
			*7.20s				7.50s
			*7.25	7.41	7.46	7.53	7.59
		7.45s					8.17s
7.31s	7.35s	7.55s	8.01s	8.15s	8.20s	8.27s	8.33s
7.43w	7.47w	7.51w					8.23w
7.43w	7.47w	7.55w	8.01w	8.15w	8.20w	8.27w	8.33w
7.54w	7.59w	8.04w	8.10w	8.24w	8.29w	8.36w*	8.42w
8.15	8.19						8.55
8.25	8.30	8.34	8.40	8.54	8.59	9.06	9.12
9.06	9.11	9.15	9.21	9.35	9.40	9.47	9.53
9.41	9.46	9.50	9.56	10.10	10.15	10.22	10.28
10.16	10.21	10.25	10.31	10.45	10.50	10.57	11.03
10.51	10.56	11.00	11.06	11.20	11.25	11.32	11.38
11.26	11.31	11.35	11.41	11.55	12.00	12.07	12.13
12.01	12.06	12.10	12.16	12.30	12.35	12.42	12.48
12.36	12.41	12.45	12.51	1.05	1.10	1.17	1.23
1.07w	1.12w	1.16w	1.22w	1.36w	1.41w	1.48w	1.54w
1.11s	1.16s	1.20s	1.26s	1.40s	1.45s	1.52s	1.58s
1.44	1.49	1.53	1.59	2.13	2.18	2.25	2.31
2.19	2.24	2.28	2.34	2.48	2.53	3.00	3.06
2.59	3.04	3.08	3.14	3.28	3.33	3.40	3.48
			*3.45w				4.15w
			*3.50w				4.20w
			*3.56w	4.12w	4.17w	4.24w	4.30w
3.44s	3.48s	3.52s	3.58s	4.12s	4.17s	4.24s	4.30s
		4.15w					4.47w
4.14	4.19	4.25	4.31	4.45	4.50	4.57	5.03
4.45w	4.49w						5.25w
4.50	4.54	4.59	5.05	5.19	5.24	5.31	5.37
4.55	5.00	5.04	5.10	5.24	5.29	5.36	5.42
5.37	5.42	5.46	5.52	6.06	6.11	6.18	6.24
6.12	6.17	6.21	6.27	6.41	6.46	6.53	6.59
6.47	6.52	6.56	7.02	7.16	7.21	7.28	7.34
7.22	7.27	7.31	7.37	7.51	7.56	8.03	8.09
7.57	8.02	8.06	8.12	8.26	8.31	8.38	8.44
8.32	8.37	8.41	8.47	9.01	9.06	9.13	9.19
9.02	9.07	9.11	9.17	9.31	9.36	9.43	9.49
9.42	9.47	9.51	9.57	10.11	10.16	10.23	10.29
10.12	10.17	10.21	10.27	10.41	10.46	10.53	10.59
10.39	10.44	10.48	10.54	11.08	11.12	11.18	11.23
			*11.45w				12.15w
			*11.55w	12.11w	12.16w	12.23w	12.29w
11.43s	11.47s	11.51s	11.57s	12.11s	12.16s	12.23s	12.29s
		12.15w					12.47w
12.09	12.14	12.25	12.31	12.45	12.50	12.57	1.03
12.45w	12.49w						1.25w
12.55	1.00	1.04	1.10	1.24	1.29	1.36	1.42

2

The Shipyard Railway cars were built in 1911, by the Wasson Car Company for the Interborough Rapid Transit Company of New York City, an elevated railroad with platform loading. On the Shipyard Railway the cars were equipped with metal folding steps, a steel pilot, and a pantograph which replaced the third-rail current collection system. (ABOVE) Trains are lined up on Richmond street awaiting the shift change at the shipyards. Trains only ran for the accommodation of shipyard workers. (LEFT) Shipyard Railway cars No. 580 and 578 near 40th & San Pablo in Emeryville. The Key System tower may be seen in the background. — BOTH CHARLES D. SAVAGE

Riding the Shipyard Railway was truly an adventure. Besides the hard rattan seats, and the rough secondhand tracks, the decrepit and loose wooden cars seemed like they were falling apart as the trains made their way back and forth between Emeryville and Richmond. (ABOVE) A six-car train, bound for Richmond as an "Express," rolls north along San Pablo Avenue in 1944. Note the lack of automobiles on the street. (RIGHT) At one of the shift changes, a train full of shipyard workers, bound for Emeryville, skips along on the outskirts of Richmond. The train is so loaded that men are riding on the outside platform. — Both Charles D. Savage

Leaving Emeryville, the Shipyard Railway ran north on San Pablo Avenue, then swung over to 9th Street and used the former Interurban Electric right-of-way through Berkeley and Albany. Where 9th Street ended, a trestle crossover was built carrying the Shipyard Railway over the Southern Pacific main line. In this scene, a five-car train crosses the SP tracks which can be seen at the right. Near the end of operation, yellow reflective stripes were painted on the sides of the gray cars. One of the Shipyard Railway cars is preserved at the Western Railway Museum at Suisun City, California. — Charles D. Savage

Westbound Sacramento Northern train No. 3, the *San Francisco Passenger*, rolls down Shafter Avenue in Oakland during October 1930. The conductor is riding the step of the lead car as the train pulls into the 40th and Shafter station. — DONALD DUKE COLLECTION

Acknowledgments

If you read the dedication to this volume, you would have noticed that it was given in the name of Charles D. Savage. His spectacular photographs of interurban trains in action appear in both volumes of *Electric Railways Around San Francisco Bay*. For his contribution to the photographic mastery of these two volumes, all I can say is "Thank God for Charles D. Savage." He was out there with camera in hand, when only a handful of railroad buffs were taking pictures. Each and every one of his photographs was a masterpiece.

Who was Charles D. Savage? I am sure the name means nothing to almost everyone who has looked over these two volumes. He was the wire chief of Western Union for the Western United States and he resided in San Francisco. What a Wire Chief is I do not know, but his job was to go out and check lines. He was a quiet man, and almost none of his photographs have ever appeared in books or magazines.

I first made contact with him in the late 1930's. While reading the "Switch List" in *Railroad Magazine* I ran onto his exchange of photographs. In those days the big deal was to trade photographs. He stated he would like to trade interurban photographs or he would sell prints. I wrote, we traded, and we became fast friends. We traded for nearly six years. I am sure I got the best of the deal, because as a kid my print quality was not that great. We had to give up trading while I was in college, but we continued to correspond. Over the years I think I gathered together some 300 of his photographs from all over the West. Savage stated he began to take photographs in the mid-1930's and finally hung up his camera in the mid-1950's. Most interurban lines were gone by that time.

Savage took mostly photographs of interurban trains. He did take a few streetcars, and only one action picture of a steam train. While at Stockton waiting for a shot of the Central California Traction to roll by, Western Pacific's *Exposition Flyer* steamed along. So he took a picture of it. If I am not mistaken, he told me his camera was a Kodak *Monitor* which used 116 size film.

For the eye-appealing variety of illustrations presented in this volume, I am grateful to the late Art Alter, Harre Demoro, Jack Hammond, Dick Jenevin, Ernest M. Leo, Joe Moir, Don Shelburne, and Richard H. Young. To those who still occasionally take a photograph once in a while, many thanks to Tom Gray, Arthur Lloyd, William D. Middleton, George White, and Will Whittaker. I would also like to thank Albert Tolf for those memorable cartoon drawings of the Market Street Railway which originally appeared first in the *San Francisco News*, as well as, his book *This was San Francisco*.

I would be remiss if I did not acknowledge Arthur Lloyd and Jeff Moreau who poured over the limited text and the story captions. They checked the facts and kept me out of trouble before this volume went to press. Also special thanks to Lowell Amrine for his present day photographs of the Municipal Railway of San Francisco.

Bibliography

Books

Demoro, Harre W., *California's Electric Railways*. Glendale, Interurban Press, 1986.

Demoro, Harre W., *Electric Railway Pioneer: Commuting on the Northwestern Pacific 1903–1941*. Glendale, Interurban Press, 1983.

Demoro, Harre W., *The Key Route: Transbay Commuting by Train and Ferry*, Glendale, Interurban Press, 1985.

Hilton, George W., and Due, John F., *The Electric Interurban Railways in America*. Stanford, Stanford University Press, 1960.

Middleton, William D., *Interurban Era*. Milwaukee, Kalmbach Publishing Co., 1961.

Middleton, William D., *The Time of the Trolley*. San Marino, Golden West Books, 1987.

Middleton, William D., *Traction Classics: The Great Wood and Steel Cars*. San Marino, Golden West Books, 1983.

Miller, John Anderson, *Fares Please! From Horse-cars to Streamliners*. New York, D. Appleton-Century Company, 1941.

Moreau, Jeffrey, *MUNI Photographs*, Orangeville, Carbarn Press, 1991.

Perles, Anthony, *The People's Railway*. Glendale, Interurban Press, 1981.

Smallwood, Charles, *The White Front Cars of San Francisco*. Glendale, Interurban Press, 1978.

Swett, Ira L., *The Market Street Railway Revisited*. Los Angeles, Interurban Press, 1972.

Swett, Ira L., and Aitken, Harry C., *The Napa Route*. Glendale, Interurban Press, 1975.

Swett, Ira L., *The Sacramento Northern*. Los Angeles, Interurban Press, 1962.

Trimble, Paul C., *Interurban Railways of the Bay Area*. Fresno, Valley Publishers, 1977.

Periodicals and Magazines

Cross, Carol W., "The San Francisco & Napa Valley Railroad: Railroading Era Comes to a Close." *Western Railroader*, Volume 37, Issue No. 408, May 1974. pp. 4-7.

Demoro, Harre W., "North Shore Railroad: Marin County Electrification." *Western Railroader*, Volume 28, Issue No. 308, September 1965. pp. 2-24.

_______________, "The Sacramento Northern." National Railway Historical Society – *The Bulletin*, Volume 37, No. 6, 1972. pp. 8-57.

_______________, "What we Saved." National Railway Historical Society – *The Bulletin*, Volume 35 No. 2, 1970. pp. 52-53.

Guido, Francis, "Napa Valley Route." *Western Railroader*, Volume 16, Issue No. 160, February 1953. pp. 2-5.

_______________, "San Mateo Suburban Line." *Western Railroader*, Volume 38, Issue No. 423, August 1975. pp. 1-8.

_______________, "The 40-line." *Western Railroader*, Volume 39, Issue No. 433, July 1976. pp. 1-8.

Heise, C.E., "The Oakland, Antioch & Eastern Railway." *Western Railroader*, Volume 34, Issue No. 382, December 1971. pp. 2-11.

Maurer, Jim, "San Francisco Municipal Railway Trolley Car Trip." *NRHS-R&LHS Convention*, June 26, 1999.

Perry, Jack E., and Townley, Robert P., "The San Francisco Municipal Railway." *Western Railroader*, Volume 28, Issue No. 300, January 1965. pp. 2-13.

Sievers, Waldemar, "Electric Interurban Service of Marin County." *Western Railroader*, Volume 17, Issue No. 178, October 1984. pp. 2-7.

Golden
West
Books